# MODERN
# Flexitarian

# MODERN
# Flexitarian

PLANT-INSPIRED RECIPES YOU CAN FLEX TO ADD FISH, MEAT, OR DAIRY

# Contents

# Beginning a Flexitarian Diet

Getting started is easier than you may think. These simple tips will help with your first steps into flexitarianism, with nutritional information to ensure you're eating a balanced diet as well as pantry suggestions and an example meal plan to make cooking easier.

# What is a flexitarian diet?

"Flexitarian" was coined more than 20 years ago to refer to people who are predominantly vegetarian, but occasionally include meat or fish in their diet. For that reason, a flexitarian diet can also be referred to as a "semi-vegetarian" diet. More recently, as people are becoming increasingly aware of the benefits of a completely plant-based diet, a number of flexitarians also consciously reduce their intake of other animal products, such as dairy and eggs.

Flexitarianism is a lifestyle choice, not another temporary fad diet. People's motivations for adopting a flexitarian diet differ (see page 12), but generally relate to their health or to a concern for animal welfare or the environment.

A flexitarian diet is about so much more than just omitting the meat from your meals; it's about making smarter food choices in general. Emphasizing good quality, minimally processed foods from sustainable sources—which are not only better for your health but for the environment, too—increases the nutrient density of your diet, thereby boosting your intake of essential vitamins, minerals, and beneficial phytochemicals from plant-based foods.

Starting a flexitarian diet is exciting and will introduce you to a whole range of plant-based alternatives to meat, including beans, lentils, and soy products (such as tofu and tempeh). Therefore, rather than seeing a flexitarian diet as restrictive or limiting, view it as an opportunity to expand your culinary horizons to a new world of delicious dishes that you and your family will love.

A common question people ask is about the amount of meat considered appropriate to include in a flexitarian diet. The great thing about this diet is the lack of rules—it's entirely up to you how often you choose to include meals with meat in your diet. To reap the maximum health benefits, you would ideally want to aim to reduce your meat intake to one serving per week, but the only commitments you need to make to call yourself a flexitarian are to consciously reduce your meat intake and to embrace more plant-based meals.

**A flexitarian diet includes:**
- Dairy products, such as cow's milk, yogurt, and cheese*
- Eggs*
- Legumes (pulses), such as chickpeas and lentils
- Vegetables
- Fruits
- Nuts and seeds
- Whole grains and their products, such as brown rice, pasta, and bread

*People who follow a flexitarian diet may also choose to reduce their intake of dairy and eggs.

**A flexitarian diet occasionally includes:**
- Red meats, such as beef and lamb
- Poultry, such as chicken and turkey
- Fish and seafood, such as salmon, tuna, and shrimp

**A flexitarian diet minimizes:**
- Processed meats, including bacon, salami, and ham
- Refined grains, such as white rice
- Refined grain products, such as white bread, cookies, and cakes
- Added sugars, particularly white sugar
- Fast foods, particularly fried foods such as french fries
- Processed snack foods, such as potato chips

# Why go flexitarian?

One of the best things about flexitarianism is that it is not a stressful lifestyle change. As a flexitarian, you can pick and choose when to eat only plant-based foods or when to add animal products, as it suits you. Additionally, every time you do enjoy a plant-based meal, you're making a positive contribution to your health and the environment, as well as reducing the negative impact of your food choices on animals. It can be cheaper, too!

## Health benefits

Many flexitarian staple foods are packed with dietary fiber, which helps keep the digestive system healthy. Unprocessed plant-based foods including fruits, vegetables, whole grains, legumes, nuts, and seeds, are all good sources of both soluble and insoluble dietary fiber, while prebiotic fiber (which promotes the growth of beneficial bacteria in the gut) can be found in pulses such as chickpeas and lentils, whole grains such as barley and rye, and a diverse range of vegetables such as onions, garlic, artichokes, and asparagus. Animal products, on the other hand, contain very little dietary fiber.

By being flexitarian and eating a balanced amount of meat, you may also help reduce your chances of developing certain cancers. The World Health Organization (WHO) has classified red meat as a Group 2A carcinogen, meaning that there is enough evidence to suggest that it probably causes cancer of the bowel and colon, while processed meats (such as hot dogs and salami) are classified as Group 1 carcinogens, which means there is convincing evidence that they cause cancer. Meanwhile, large population studies have shown that predominantly plant-based diets—including semi-vegetarian diets—are associated with a lower risk of developing colorectal cancer.

In addition, diets rich in fruits and vegetables, whole grains, legumes, and nuts are consistently associated with a lower risk of developing type 2 diabetes. By limiting your red meat and poultry intake and instead choosing plant-based meals made up of legumes, vegetables, and whole grains, you'll reduce your risk of developing type 2 diabetes.

## Environmental benefits

Our current global food production system is the single largest driver of environmental degradation, contributing to climate change, biodiversity loss, and unsustainable land and water use. To conserve the health of the planet while feeding a growing global population that is projected to reach 10 billion people by 2050, a team of scientists from the EAT-Lancet Commission—an organization of 37 diet and food sustainability experts—have called for a global shift to a flexitarian-style "planetary health diet." This diet consists of fruits, vegetables, whole grains, nuts, seeds, plant proteins (including beans and lentils), and unsaturated plant oils; it includes only modest amounts of meat and dairy.

## Cost benefits

Whether you are moving to a flexitarian, vegetarian, or vegan diet, there are hidden costs that can develop, especially if you're relying on premade meals and processed foods. But this doesn't need to be the case. Being flexitarian is arguably cheaper than regularly eating meat or fish, as these are the most expensive items on a standard shopping list. Expensive convenience items—such as faux meats—can be easily avoided by learning how to prepare pulses and tofu so they're appealing and delicious. Before you know it, you will have a pantry full of canned or dried pulses, whole grains, nuts, and seeds, as well as fresh fruits and vegetables, that you can rely on to build weekly meals on a budget.

## Animal welfare benefits

The production of meat, dairy, or eggs is a business and, like any other, it must be profitable in order to survive. Animal welfare concerns can often be sacrificed in order to keep costs for consumers down, which for many people is a key reason for choosing to reduce their intake of animal products. If and when you do buy meat, fish, and eggs, look for organic certification, which should be an indicator of good quality and higher welfare standards.

# How to be flexitarian

As the word suggests, the great thing about flexitarianism is its flexibility. If you're trying to go flexitarian for the first time, you have the freedom to make as many or as few changes as you feel comfortable with, and take it from there. Here are some tips and inspiration to help you get started and stay on track.

• Start small. Commit to just one meat-free day per week, such as "Meatless Monday," and steadily adjust your diet from there.

• If you're finding it tricky to adjust from the traditional "meat and potatoes" idea of mealtimes, make the most of meat-alternative products. Supermarkets now stock a wide selection of vegetarian and vegan options that have a similar taste and texture to meat, including burgers, sausages, and faux chicken fillets and nuggets. While they aren't as nutrient-rich as unprocessed whole foods like beans and lentils, they're a great option when you're adjusting to meat-free meals.

• Instead of cutting meat from your meals entirely, try substituting half the meat content for a plant-based source of protein, such as beans or lentils. For instance, you could bulk up your spaghetti Bolognese with brown lentils, which will boost the fiber and phytochemical content of the dish significantly. This fifty–fifty approach allows you to halve your red meat intake while still enjoying the flavor and textures you love.

• If you feel held back by your cooking skills or are stuck for ideas, seek out a local vegetarian or vegan cooking class to boost your kitchen confidence. You could also visit a local vegan restaurant to familiarize yourself with the range of tastes and textures plant-based cooking can offer. Taste a few dishes, then try recreating your favorites at home.

• Include your friends and family in your new diet by hosting a plant-based dinner. Who knows? You might inspire them to go flexitarian, too.

• Take inspiration from cuisines that traditionally use beans and lentils, and bring out their flavor with herbs and spices. Try a hearty Mediterranean soup or stew that uses beans; an Indian dhal or curry with lentils, peas, or chickpeas; or a Mexican chili that makes the most of kidney or pinto beans.

• Prepare large batches of your favorite plant-based recipes, then freeze the leftovers or save them for lunch the following day. That way, if you're short on time, you won't get caught without a flexitarian option on hand.

• Sit down on Sunday and plan the week's meals ahead. This will help you save time and money, and minimize food waste. See pages 26–27 for a sample weekly meal plan.

# A balanced flexitarian diet

When making any dietary change, it's important to be aware of how it will impact your day-to-day nutritional intake. For example, if you decide to omit dairy products from your diet, you need to make sure you're still meeting your body's needs for key nutrients that dairy once provided, such as calcium, iodine, and vitamin B12. If you think you may benefit from one-on-one dietary advice, speak to a dietitian or doctor who can help you plan your new diet to ensure you are meeting your personal nutritional needs.

## The five food groups

Outlined below and opposite are five food groups that each provide similar amounts of key nutrients per serving. The foods listed within these groups will make up the core of your flexitarian diet. While it is important that you are including the recommended number of servings from the five food groups each day, you should also try to include a variety of foods from within each group, as different foods within the same groups differ in their nutrient content. There is an endless number of delicious meals you can create by combining foods from all the food groups. By doing so, you'll be able to make healthy food choices effortlessly, as these whole and minimally processed foods retain most of their original nutritional content.

The information given here is based on an average adult diet. The recommended daily number of servings of each food group will differ for toddlers, children, teenagers, and those who are pregnant or breastfeeding. Consult ChooseMyPlate.gov for the most accurate advice.

*Servings per day*

**Adults 5–6**

### Vegetables and legumes
You can't eat too many vegetables! Vegetables, legumes, and beans are a good source of folic acid, fiber, vitamin C, potassium, and magnesium. They also provide a range of beneficial phytochemicals, so try to eat a varied and colorful range of vegetables each day.

1 serving, containing around 25–85 cal, is roughly equal to:

- ½ cup (75g) cooked vegetables such as broccoli, corn, spinach, pumpkin, or carrots
- ½ cup (75g) cooked dried or canned beans, peas, or lentils
- 1 cup (75g) green leafy or raw salad vegetables
- ½ medium potato or other starchy vegetables, such as sweet potato
- 1 medium tomato

*Servings per day*

**Adults 2**

### Fruit
A serving of fruit provides a good source of folic acid, dietary fiber, vitamin C, provitamin A carotenoids, potassium, and magnesium. Some fruits can also contain a range of beneficial phytochemicals, such as the antioxidants found in berries.

1 serving, containing around 85 cal, is roughly equal to:

- 1 medium piece of fruit, such as an apple, orange, or banana
- 2 small pieces of fruit, such as kiwis, plums, or apricots
- 5½oz (150g) diced fruit, such as pineapple or mango (including fruit canned in natural juice)

A 1oz (30g) portion of dried fruit, such as raisins or dried apricots, or ½ cup (120ml) of fruit juice (with no added sugar) can also count as one serving of fruit, but only occasionally as these choices can increase the risk of tooth decay.

**Adults
3–6**

### Starchy, grain-based foods
Starchy foods should make up just over a third of every meal you eat, as they help satisfy your hunger and are a good source of carbohydrates, protein, dietary fiber, magnesium, B vitamins, vitamin E, phosphorous, iron, and zinc. It's important to choose whole grain or whole wheat foods wherever possible, rather than highly refined and processed varieties, such as white bread. Refined grains have been stripped of germ and bran layers, which significantly reduces their vitamin, mineral, and antioxidant content.

1 serving, containing around 120 cal, is roughly equal to:

- 1 slice (1½oz/40g) bread
- ½ medium (1½oz/40g) bread roll or flatbread
- ½ cup (75–120g) cooked rice or other grains, such as pasta, noodles, couscous, polenta, or semolina
- ½ cup (120g) cooked oatmeal
- ⅔ cup (30g) bran flakes
- ¼ cup (30g) muesli or rolled oats

**Adults
2–3**

### Lean meat, poultry, fish, eggs, nuts, seeds, and legumes
On a flexitarian diet, you'll automatically be eating less meat, poultry, fish, and eggs. Luckily, the plant-based options in this food group also provide a good source of protein, iron, and zinc. However, while meat, fish, and eggs are all good sources of vitamin B12, the plant foods in this group are not. See page 20 for more information about vitamin B12 to ensure you're getting the right amount on a flexitarian diet.

1 serving, containing around 120–145 cal, is roughly equal to:

- 2⅛oz (65g) cooked lean red meat (3¼–3½oz/90–100g raw)
- 2¾oz (80g) cooked poultry (3½oz/100g raw)
- 3½oz (100g) cooked fish (4oz/115g raw) or 1 small can of fish
- 2 large eggs
- 1 cup (150g) cooked legumes (dried or canned)
- 6oz (170g) firm tofu
- 1oz (30g) nuts or seeds, or their pastes or butters (only occasionally as they provide fewer nutrients)

Experts recommend that you eat no more than 7 servings of red meat per week. This shouldn't be too much of an issue on a flexitarian diet, as you'll already be aiming to cut back on red meat.

### Milk, yogurt, cheese, and their alternatives
This food group contains a variety of dairy and nondairy options, which caters perfectly to a flexitarian diet. Milk, yogurt, cheese, and their alternatives are a good source of protein and calcium. While dairy products are also an important source of the mineral iodine, dairy alternatives—such as soy milk and tofu—are not. See page 21 for more information about iodine.

**Adults
2½–4**

1 serving, containing around 120–145 cal, is roughly equal to:

- 1 cup (250ml) cow's milk or calcium-fortified nondairy milk
- 1½oz (40g) hard cheese
- ½ cup (120g) soft cheese, such as ricotta
- ¾ cup (200g) yogurt
- 3½oz (100g) calcium-set firm tofu (check ingredients for calcium sulfate E516 or calcium chloride E509)
- 2oz (60g) canned sardines
- 3½oz (100g) canned pink salmon with bones

It is recommended you choose reduced-fat varieties of milk, yogurt, and soft cheese, and keep your hard cheese intake to around two or three servings per week. Keep in mind that reduced-fat varieties of dairy products are not suitable for children under the age of two due to their high energy needs for growth. Infants (aged under 12 months) should not be given cow's milk as a main drink; breast milk or formula is recommended as the main source of milk.

### "Sometimes" foods

You may wonder where cake, pastries, ice cream, chocolate, chips, alcohol, and other processed and fast foods sit within these five food groups. The straight answer is that they don't. These are discretionary foods, and are not necessary for a healthy diet because they don't provide important nutrients. That being said, occasionally including these foods in your diet—in small amounts—doesn't pose a risk to health. A good way to think of these foods is as "sometimes" foods.

# Macronutrients

Protein, carbohydrates, and fat are the three main macronutrients that the body needs in large amounts to provide it with energy. When adopting a flexitarian diet, you may be worried about getting enough protein because you'll be reducing your intake of meat, fish, and eggs (which are commonly thought of as protein foods) and increasing your intake of foods such as beans and lentils (which are commonly considered carbohydrates). Unfortunately, this view is overly simplistic, as most whole foods—unlike those that are highly processed—actually provide a combination of protein, carbohydrates, and fat. For example, two slices of a good-quality whole wheat bread, often considered to be purely a source of carbohydrates, actually provide 11 grams of protein and 5 grams of fat, as well as 19 grams of carbohydrate.

## Carbohydrates

Our bodies obtain energy in the form of glucose from carbohydrates. Glucose fuels our body's cells, powering our brain and muscles. Carbohydrates are predominantly found in plant foods, with the exception of the sugar lactose, which is found in dairy products. Below are foods with good sources of carbohydrates to include daily in your flexitarian diet.

- Fruits, such as bananas, apples, and berries
- Vegetables, particularly starchy vegetables such as potatoes, sweet potatoes, and corn
- Whole grains, including brown rice, quinoa, and oats, and whole grain products, such as bread, pasta, and noodles
- Pulses, including beans, peas, chickpeas, and lentils

## Protein

This vital macronutrient is important for tissue building and repair; growth and maintenance of muscle mass; and the maintenance of healthy, strong bones. Protein is made up of twenty amino acids, nine of which are essential, which means that they can't be made by the body and must be obtained through the diet. The foods listed below are all good sources of protein and contain all nine essential amino acids for you to include in your daily diet.

Animal foods

- 2⅛oz (65g) cooked lean meat, such as lean beef, lamb, or pork (provides 20-22g of protein)
- 2¾oz (80g) cooked poultry, such as skinless grilled chicken breast (provides 24g of protein)
- 3½oz (100g) cooked white or oily fish, such as salmon or cod (provides 22-24g of protein)
- 2 large eggs (provides 12g of protein)

Plant foods

- 6oz (170g) firm tofu (provides 20g of protein)
- 3½oz (100g) tempeh (provides 18g of protein)
- 1 cup (150g) cooked legumes, such as beans, peas, chickpeas, and lentils (provides 10-12g of protein)

If you choose to omit fish from your diet, plant-derived omega-3 supplements are available, made from microalgae.

## Fats

A certain amount of fat is essential for the body to function; it is a concentrated source of energy and it aids the absorption of fat-soluble nutrients, including vitamins A and E. There are two main types of dietary fats: saturated and unsaturated. Saturated fats—found mostly in animal products—are associated with negative health effects, and so should be limited. The beauty of a flexitarian diet is that by reducing your meat intake, you'll be reducing your intake of saturated fat, not to mention cholesterol. The healthier unsaturated fats play an important part in a flexitarian diet and are associated with health benefits. Below are some good sources of these healthy unsaturated fats, but keep in mind that unless you have high energy needs or need to gain weight, your body doesn't need an overly large amount of fats, even the healthy ones.

- Nuts and seeds, such as sunflower seeds, pumpkin seeds, almonds, and walnuts
- Whole grains, such as rolled oats
- Soy products, including tofu, tempeh, and soy milk
- Oily fish, such as salmon
- Avocados
- Olive oil and other vegetable oils

It is also important to ensure that your diet includes good sources of the essential omega-3 fatty acids ALA, EPA, and DHA. ALA is found in good amounts in walnuts, chia seeds, and flaxseeds, whereas oily fish is the richest dietary source of EPA and DHA.

# Vitamins

We are unable to synthesize vitamins in our body and so must obtain these essential nutrients—needed only in small amounts—through our diet. On a flexitarian diet, it's important to make sure you're paying attention to the following vitamins, which can fall short when your meat and dairy intakes are reduced.

### Vitamin A
Important for vision, healthy skin, iron metabolism, and immune-system function, vitamin A has two types: preformed vitamin A, which is primarily found in dairy products, and provitamin A, which exists in many vegetables as carotenoids that our bodies are able to convert to the active form of vitamin A. Vegetables rich in provitamin A carotenoids (such as beta carotene) include carrots, sweet potatoes, pumpkins, kale, spinach, and red peppers.

### Vitamin D
Foods such as oily fish, eggs, and fortified milks do contain some vitamin D, but the majority of vitamin D required by the body is derived from safe sun exposure. Depending on where you live, it might be a good idea to take a vitamin D supplement through the cooler months of the year, when UV levels are low. Speak to your doctor or a dietitian for more information about an appropriate supplement for you.

### Vitamin B$_{12}$
Our bodies receive the important vitamin B$_{12}$ from animal foods in our diet. Vitamin B$_{12}$ is required for cell division, blood formation, neurological structure and function, energy metabolism, psychological function, and immunity. Because plant foods don't contain vitamin B$_{12}$, if you've reduced your meat and dairy intake you may need to take a vitamin B$_{12}$ supplement to ensure you're meeting your body's daily requirement. Certain brands of specialty foods such as soy milk and vegetarian sausages are fortified with the vitamin, meaning it has been added by the manufacturer. However, three servings of these fortified foods are required every day in order to meet the body's needs. Speak to your doctor or a dietitian for more information.

# Minerals

Like vitamins, minerals are must-have nutrients which we are unable to synthesize in our body and must obtain through our diet. They are inorganic elements which are classified into two groups: major minerals which are required in larger amounts, such as calcium and potassium, and trace elements which are required in smaller amounts, such as iron and zinc. By eating a balanced flexitarian diet, you can easily meet your body's mineral requirements, but it's worth making sure you eat good sources of calcium, iron, zinc, and iodine.

### Calcium
This mineral is essential for nerve and muscle function, blood coagulation, energy metabolism, and to keep bones and teeth healthy and strong. It is most commonly known to be sourced from dairy products, but there are plenty of plant-based sources for those who wish to reduce their daily consumption.

Animal foods that contain calcium

- 1 cup (250ml) cow's milk (provides 320mg of calcium)
- 1 cup (200g) yogurt (provides 340mg of calcium)
- ½oz (40g) hard cheese (provides 320mg of calcium)
- 3½oz (100g) canned pink salmon (provides 190mg of calcium)

Plant foods that contain calcium

- 1 cup (250ml) calcium-fortified nondairy milk (provides 300mg of calcium)
- 6oz (175g) calcium-set tofu (provides 240mg of calcium)
- 1 cup (150g) cooked Asian greens, such as bok choy (provides 125mg of calcium)
- 1 cup (150g) cooked kale (provides 100mg of calcium)
- 1 cup (150g) cooked legumes, such as chickpeas (provides 68mg of calcium)

## Iron

Many people rely on red meat for their iron needs, although there are many notable sources of iron from plant foods. Iron is vital for transporting oxygen around the body, energy production, immunity, blood formation, and cognitive function.

Animal foods that contain iron

- 2⅛oz (65g) cooked beef, such as lean rump steak (provides 2.2mg of iron)
- 2⅛oz (65g) cooked lamb, such as lean rump steak (provides 2mg of iron)
- 2¾oz (80g) cooked poultry, such as skinless grilled chicken breast (provides 0.6mg of iron)

Plant foods that contain iron

- 6oz (170g) firm tofu (provides 4.9mg of iron)
- 1 cup (150g) legumes, including beans, peas, chickpeas, and lentils (provides 2–3mg of iron)
- 3½oz (100g) tempeh (provides 2.7mg of iron)
- ⅓ cup (75g) cooked spinach (provides 2.7mg of iron)
- ½ cup (60g) rolled oats (provides 2.1mg of iron)
- 1 cup (150g) cooked quinoa (provides 1.9mg of iron)
- 2oz (30g) nuts, such as cashews (provides 1.5mg of iron)

The body's absorption of iron from plant foods can be boosted by ensuring iron-rich meals include a good source of vitamin C, such as peppers, tomatoes, or broccoli. Just as iron absorption by the body can be enhanced by vitamin C, it can also be inhibited by phenolic compounds in coffee and black tea, so avoid drinking these with your iron-rich main meals to optimize iron absorption.

## Zinc

This mineral performs critical functions in the body, including keeping your immune system in good shape and maintaining healthy skin, hair, and nails. The absorption of zinc is inhibited by phytates, which are compounds found in legumes, whole grains, nuts, and seeds. Not to worry: phytates can be deactivated by food preparation methods including soaking, sprouting (germination), and fermentation, so choosing foods such as whole wheat sourdough bread (which has been fermented) and sprouted seeds will optimize your zinc uptake from meals. The following are good sources of zinc to include in your diet:

Animal foods that contain zinc

- ½oz (15g) fresh oysters (provides 55mg of zinc)
- 2⅛oz (65g) cooked beef, such as lean rump steak (provides 5.3mg of zinc)
- 2⅛oz (65g) cooked lamb, such as lean rump steak (provides 3.8mg of zinc)
- 2¾oz (80g) cooked poultry, such as skinless grilled chicken breast (provides 0.5mg of zinc)

Plant foods that contain zinc

- 6oz (170g) firm tofu (provides 2.9mg of zinc)
- 1oz (30g) seeds, such as pepitas (provides 2.2mg of zinc)
- 1oz (30g) nuts, such as cashews (provides 1.6mg of zinc)
- 1 cup (150g) cooked legumes, including beans, peas, chickpeas, and lentils (provides 1–1.5mg of zinc)
- ½ cup (60g) rolled oats (provides 1.4mg of zinc)
- 3½oz (100g) tempeh (provides 1.1mg of zinc)

Pumpkin seeds (pepitas) are a good plant food source of zinc, so get into the habit of sprinkling sprouted pumpkin seeds on your meals to boost your zinc intake.

## Iodine

The mineral iodine is important for thyroid function, energy metabolism, and cognitive function. Most people get a significant proportion of their daily iodine intake from dairy foods, so if you're ditching dairy—particularly cow's milk—it's important to make sure you're getting enough from other sources. Plant foods (with the exception of seaweeds) are a poor source of iodine. A daily multivitamin supplement can be an easy way to ensure you're meeting your iodine needs, which is particularly important if you're planning a pregnancy. Speak to your doctor or a dietitian for more information. Here are some good sources of iodine to incorporate into your diet:

Animal foods that contain iodine

- 3½oz (100g) fresh oysters (provides 185mcg of iodine)
- 1 cup (250ml) cow's milk (provides 60mcg of iodine)
- 2 large eggs (provides 58mcg of iodine)
- 3½oz (105g) canned pink salmon (provides 50mcg of iodine)
- 1 cup (200g) yogurt (provides 24mcg of iodine)

Plant foods that contain iodine

- ¼ teaspoon (1.5g) iodized salt (provides 66mcg of iodine)
- 2 slices (1¼oz/33g) wheat bread, fortified with iodized salt (provides 33mcg of iodine)

# Simple swaps

Going flexitarian involves finding new plant-based favorites to replace the animal products you might have once consumed every day. You may not want to swap out every dairy product in your fridge for a vegan equivalent just yet, but even one or two substitutions will help you toward your personal flexitarian goal. Take a look at this list of healthy plant-based options for common food and drink items to find the right products for you.

## Dairy milk substitutes

**Soy milk** is made by blending boiled soy beans with water and various additives, such as sugar and calcium. Soy milk has a creamy texture and is great for drinking straight or adding to smoothies or cereal. It is also good in tea or coffee as it doesn't split at high temperatures. For this reason, it's also a good choice for cooking and baking. Soy milk is nutritionally the most similar to cow's milk, with around 7 grams of protein per cup (250ml), but it doesn't contain high amounts of calcium, unless added by the manufacturer, so be sure to check the label.

**Unsweetened almond milk** is a good alternative to dairy milk in cooking and baking, as well as in smoothies, on cereal, or drinking plain. However, it might add a slight sweetness to savory dishes (despite the name). Almond milk is produced by blending almonds with water. Not all almond milks are fortified with calcium, so it's important to check the label. Unlike soy milk, almond milk is not a good source of protein.

**Unsweetened drinking coconut milk** can be drunk on its own, added to cereal, or used in cooking. It is made by combining coconut milk or cream with water, and is found with other milks in supermarkets. It is not nutrient-rich unless fortified by the manufacturer.

**Oat milk** is made by blending soaked oats and water. It has a slightly viscous texture and mild, sweet taste. It is suitable for drinking plain, in smoothies, and in most cooked dishes, except for those that need to be gluten-free. Oat milk is a good source of fiber and also contains the soluble fiber beta-glucan, which is clinically proven to help reduce bad cholesterol levels. It's also a good option for people who have soy or nut allergies.

**Rice milk** is just rice and water, and has a thin texture due to its low protein content. It's a tasty addition in smoothies or on cereal due to its naturally sweet taste, but it is a significant source of carbohydrates, containing about 30 grams per cup (250ml). It is another good option for people who have soy or nut allergies.

## Butter substitutes

**Vegetable oil spreads** are ideal for spreading, cooking, or baking. They are a good source of vitamin E, healthy unsaturated fats (including omega-6), and are often fortified with vitamins A and D. They can be used as a substitute for butter weight for weight in recipes. If you are avoiding dairy, be sure to check the label as certain brands contain milk solids.

## Cheese substitutes

**Nutritional yeast** offers a savory cheese flavor to dishes and is a useful cheese alternative for stirring into risottos and sauces, or for sprinkling over pasta. It is a source of protein and fiber, and is fortified with B vitamins.

**Nut cheeses** are a blend of nuts and water with a nondairy probiotic added to ferment the cheese. They are great to use as spreads and to add to cooked dishes, such as lasagna.

You might have noticed the variety of commercial vegan cheeses available in your supermarket. These are usually made with highly processed ingredients, such as soy protein and starches, with the addition of colors and flavors, and are not usually a good source of micronutrients. Of course, you might decide to include these faux cheeses occasionally, but they aren't essential components of a healthy flexitarian diet.

## Honey substitutes

**Agave nectar** is a natural sweetener and has a similar texture to honey. You can swap the honey quantity in a recipe for the same amount of agave.

**Rice malt syrup** is made from brown rice, giving it a rich flavor with a mild sweetness. It can be substituted for the same amount of honey in recipes.

**Maple syrup** has a slightly stronger flavor than agave nectar or rice malt syrup. It is great for drizzling and can be substituted for the same amount of honey in recipes. Be sure to purchase pure maple syrup and not an artificial maple-flavored syrup. Maple syrup can be quite expensive, but a little goes a long way.

## Meat and seafood substitutes

**Tofu** is produced by curdling and pressing soy milk. It has a neutral taste and absorbs the flavor of whatever it is marinated or cooked with. Firm tofu is good for using in stir-fries and soups because it keeps its structure, while silken tofu is perfect for making sauces, dressings, and smoothies because it is delicate and falls apart easily. Tofu is a good source of protein, iron, and zinc—and calcium, too, if set with the addition of a calcium salt.

**Tempeh** is a traditional Indonesian food that is made by fermenting soy beans into a savory cake form. It has a strong nutty flavor and a chewy texture, making it a great addition to stir-fries. It is even higher in protein than tofu, and is a good source of iron and zinc.

**Seitan** is a non-soy product, made from vital wheat gluten and water to form a dough which is usually shaped to resemble meat or seafood and then cooked. It has a meaty and chewy texture with a similar "bite" to chicken, and can be used as a substitute for meat or fish in cooked dishes. Seitan is a good source of protein, iron, and zinc.

As well as a plethora of commercial vegan cheeses that are now available in supermarkets, you'll also notice a variety of faux meat and seafood products. These are usually highly processed and full of artificial ingredients and aren't essential to a healthy flexitarian diet.

## Egg substitutes

**Aquafaba** is the liquid that chickpeas have been cooked in, and includes the liquid from a can of chickpeas. It has emulsifying, binding, foaming, and thickening properties and is the perfect substitute for egg whites in recipes that call for beaten egg whites, such as meringues and chocolate mousse. In general, three tablespoons of aquafaba is equal to one egg.

**Chia seeds** mixed with water are a good swap for eggs in baking recipes, as the mixture works like a binding agent similar to eggs. A mixture of one tablespoon of chia seeds to three tablespoons of water is equal to one egg.

**Flax seeds** and water can be used in the same way as chia seeds to replace egg, but this mixture has a stronger and nuttier flavor.

# The flexitarian pantry

The secret to any diet change is not to be caught short, or else you can quickly revert to old ways. Flexitarianism is no different. Make sure to keep your pantry well-stocked with items such as those listed here, focusing on nutritious whole foods in their natural, unprocessed state wherever possible.

## Baking ingredients

**Baking powder and baking soda** for making cakes, cookies, brownies, and muffins.

**Cocoa or raw cacao powder** to use in baked goods, smoothies, or hot chocolate.

**Flours** such as whole wheat, all-purpose, and self-raising flours, plus gluten-free varieties (such as buckwheat) if required.

**Good-quality dark chocolate** (either in block form or as chips) to use in baking. If you're limiting your dairy intake, be sure to choose a vegan variety.

**Sweeteners**, including maple syrup, agave nectar, rice malt syrup, and raw brown sugar.

## Savory staples

**A selection of dried herbs and spices** are essential for everyday cooking. Useful ones to have on hand include bay leaves, black pepper, cayenne pepper, cinnamon, coriander, cumin, curry powder, chili, ginger, mustard seeds, nutmeg, oregano, smoked paprika, salt, thyme, turmeric, and rosemary.

**Canned black beans and kidney beans** are a good meat alternative for homemade burgers, stews, and Mexican-inspired dishes.

**Canned cannellini beans** are perfect in soups; salads; or simply mashed with garlic, lemon, and herbs to use as a spread or dip.

**Canned chickpeas** are an essential pantry item in a flexitarian diet. Affordable and a great source of protein, they can be used to whip up a quick hummus dip, to make falafel or as an addition to salads, pasta dishes, and curries.

**Canned lentils** are a nutritious replacement for ground meat in Italian recipes, such as spaghetti Bolognese, and are perfect for salads, soups, and curries.

**Dried versions** of the above legumes are cheaper than canned for when you have time to soak them prior to cooking.

**Green and yellow split peas** to add a smoky flavor to soups and dhals.

**Other legumes,** such as mung beans, borlotti beans, adzuki beans, black beans, moth beans, navy beans, pigeon peas, black-eyed peas, pinto beans, and soy beans, can be purchased as required and as you grow more confident in trying out new foods and recipes.

## Nuts, seeds, and dried fruits

**Almonds and cashews** are pantry essentials, as they are perfect for baking, making "cheese" fillings and nut milks, and for plain old snacking.

**Chia seeds and flaxseeds** can be added to oatmeal, cereal, muesli, and smoothies. Mixed with water, they act as an ideal egg replacement when baking.

**Dried fruits,** such as Medjool dates, raisins, figs, and apricots, come in handy when making muesli or baking, and they make marvelous snacks, too.

**Pumpkin, sesame, and sunflower seeds** are good garnishes to keep on hand to add a crunch to salads, soups, and stir-fries.

**Walnuts, pecans, and pine nuts** are delicious, especially when toasted first, and great to have on hand for snacking and baking.

## Oils

**Extra-virgin olive oil** (preferably cold-pressed) is perfect for drizzling over Mediterranean dishes and whisked into salad dressings. Extra-virgin olive oil has a relatively high smoke point, so should not be used for frying.

**Olive oil** is better suited to quick frying and roasting than extra-virgin olive oil (see above).

**Rapeseed oil** is light and clear with a neutral flavor; it is a good choice for quick frying.

**Coconut oil** is great in curries and baked goods, but use in moderation as it is high in saturated fat.

**Sesame oil** adds a nutty flavor to Asian dishes, and is an excellent addition to marinades and sauces.

**Sunflower and vegetable oils** have a high smoke point and are best used for deep-frying dishes.

## Grain-based foods

**Grains** such as brown rice, quinoa, bulgur wheat, freekeh, whole wheat couscous, and pearl barley.

**Rolled oats** to make oatmeal, muesli, granola, and baked goods.

**Whole grain sourdough bread** to top with healthy spreads or make sandwiches.

**Whole wheat dried pasta and ramen, soba, and rice noodles** for easy weeknight dinners.

## Staples and condiments

**Canned staples** such as whole and diced tomatoes, coconut milk, and coconut cream.

**Dried staples** such as nutritional yeast and breadcrumbs.

**Olives, pickles, capers, sun dried tomatoes, or preserved artichoke hearts** to add flavor to meals.

**Sauces and pastes,** including a good-quality homemade or store-bought tomato sauce, a hot chili sauce such as sriracha or sambal oelek, good-quality curry pastes, tomato paste, harissa paste, Worcestershire sauce, fish sauce (vegan varieties are available), hoisin sauce, salsa, soy sauce, kecap manis (sweet soy sauce), and tamari (Japanese soy sauce).

**Spreads** such as peanut butter, almond butter, tahini, Marmite, jams, marmalades, and mustard.

**Soy milk** or your other favorite plant-based nondairy milk, such as coconut, almond, or oat.

**Vinegars** for dressings and sauces, such as balsamic, apple cider, rice wine, and red wine vinegars.

## Frozen foods

**Frozen berries** are just as nutritious as fresh berries but with the convenience of staying fresher longer. Ensure you buy a brand that doesn't add sugar—check the ingredients list on the package if you are unsure.

**Frozen vegetables,** such as peas, corn, and spinach, are handy for soups and stews.

# Meal planning

A flexitarian diet is, of course, designed to be flexible. Nevertheless, getting into the habit of meal planning will make meeting your goals a lot easier. Put aside a little time each week to decide what you're going to cook (and whether they'll include meat or fish) and you'll save time and effort in the long run.

Below is a sample weekly menu made up of recipes from this book. Decide in advance which recipes will include animal products, write up a shopping list for all the ingredients you'll need, and remember to include a nutritious snack or two every day (such as a handful of nuts or a piece of fresh fruit) and your week will be full of delicious healthy food.

Freeze any leftovers and you'll soon have a freezer stocked with meals for busy weeks when your cooking time is limited.

| | Breakfast | Lunch | Dinner |
|---|---|---|---|
| **Monday** | Wheat Berry Bircher Muesli Pots (page 64) can be made in advance and will keep in the fridge for quick breakfasts or snacks throughout the week. | Savory Green Pancakes with Feta and Sprout Salad (page 88). These can be made over the weekend so they are ready for weekday lunches. | Rainbow Lentil Meatballs with Arrabbiata Sauce (page 220) |
| **Tuesday** | Spiced Apple and Mung Bean Muffins (page 58) are perfect for breakfast or snacks throughout the week. | Quinoa Falafel with Mint Yogurt Sauce (page 106) | Black-Eyed Pea Sliders with Pico de Gallo (page 94) |
| **Wednesday** | Wheat Berry Bircher Muesli Pots (page 64) | Mung Bean Gado Gado (page 120) | Lima Bean Enchiladas (page 204) |
| **Thursday** | Curried Mung Bean Avocado Toast (page 46) | Rainbow Bowl with Sesame and Ginger Dressing (page 114) | Green Minestrone with Kale and Walnut Pesto (page 152), making a double batch for lunch tomorrow. |
| **Friday** | Tropical Smoothie Bowl (page 60) | Green Minestrone with Kale and Walnut Pesto (page 152), using leftovers from last night's dinner. | Zucchini, Herb, and Lemon Tagine (page 184) |
| **Saturday** | Black Bean Breakfast Tostadas (page 54) | Avocado, Cilantro, and Lime Tabbouleh (page 124) | Brazilian Black Bean and Pumpkin Stew (page 160), making a double batch for lunch tomorrow. |
| **Sunday** | Whole Wheat Pancakes with Apple and Cinnamon (page 62) | Brazilian Black Bean and Pumpkin Stew (page 160), using leftovers from last night's dinner. | Shaved Asparagus, Mint, and Edamame Spaghetti (page 212) |

# Basics

There's nothing quite like using your own homemade basics when cooking. Make your own stock, nut milk, yogurt, fresh pasta dough, and more with these essential recipes.

# Simple Vegetable Stock

This light and flavorful vegetable stock blends well with all manner of other ingredients, making it the perfect base for any soup or sauce.

**makes** 1 gallon (4 liters)   **prep** 15 min   **cook** 2 hr

1  In a large stockpot or deep-sided large pan, combine the leeks, onions, carrots, celery, button mushrooms, bay leaf, flat-leaf parsley, thyme, peppercorns, and tamari. Cover with the filtered water.

2  Set the pan over high heat, bring to a boil, cover, reduce the heat to a gentle simmer, and cook for 2 hours.

3  Cool completely; strain and discard the vegetables, herbs, and spices; and pour the stock into glass jars or BPA-free containers for storage. Stock will keep in the fridge for up to 7 days or in the freezer for up to 3 months.

2 large leeks, halved lengthwise, washed, and cut into 1in (2.5cm) chunks

2 large yellow onions, root end trimmed and cut into 1in (2.5cm) chunks

4 carrots, scrubbed and cut into 1in (2.5cm) chunks (no need to peel)

8 large stalks celery, cut into 1in (2.5cm) chunks

2 cups (140g) sliced button mushrooms

1 bay leaf

½ cup (30g) fresh flat-leaf parsley leaves and stems

3 sprigs thyme

1 tsp whole black peppercorns

2 tbsp tamari or soy sauce

1 gallon (4 liters) filtered water

## Why not try ...

For Mushroom Stock, sauté the leeks, carrots, and celery in 2 tbsp extra-virgin olive oil for 15 minutes or until golden. Add 2 cups (140g) sliced chestnut mushrooms and a scant 1oz (25g) dried porcini mushrooms to the pan along with raw, unpeeled onions when you add water, and proceed as directed.

# Vegan Ramen Stock

This stock is light and fragrant, and will provide the perfect base for ramen. Charring the onion and ginger will increase their flavor profiles. Do it over an open flame or in a dry pan over a high heat.

**makes** 2½–2¾ pints (1.4–1.7 liters)  **prep** 15 min  **cook** 45 min

1  Heat the vegetable oil in a large pot over medium-high heat. Add the onion, celery, ginger, leeks, carrots, and garlic.

2  Stirring constantly, cook for 10 minutes to caramelize the vegetables.

3  Add the water and bring to a boil over high heat. Add the button mushrooms and spring onions, lower the heat to a simmer, and cook for 30 minutes.

4  Allow to cool to room temperature, or overnight in the fridge to allow maximum infused flavor. Strain the stock and discard the solids. Stock will keep in the fridge for up to 7 days or in the freezer for up to 3 months.

2 tbsp vegetable oil

1 large onion, roughly chopped

2 celery stalks, roughly chopped

2in (5cm) piece ginger, sliced

2 leeks, sliced and washed

2 large carrots, roughly chopped (no need to peel)

6–8 medium cloves garlic, crushed

3½ pints (2 liters) water

2½ cups (175g) roughly chopped button mushrooms

1 bunch spring onions (6–8 stems), roughly chopped

# Fresh Pasta Dough

You can easily make your own fresh pasta dough with or without eggs. For added flavor and a pretty golden color, try saffron or tomato paste—or both. Use a pasta machine to roll the dough if you have one, but a rolling pin also works well if you don't.

**serves** 4   **prep** 30 min   **cook** 3 min

1   In a small bowl, whisk the extra-virgin olive oil into the warm water. Then, whisk in the tomato paste and/or saffron (if using).

2   In a large bowl, stir together the flour and salt. Mound the flour mixture on a wooden board or clean kitchen countertop, and make a well in the center. Pour the olive oil–water mixture into the well.

3   Using a fork, slowly mix the flour mixture into the olive oil mixture, a little at a time, until nearly all has been incorporated. Knead by hand for about 5 minutes, sprinkling your work surface with flour as you work. If the dough seems dry, add more water, a few drops at a time. When you've finished kneading, you should end up with a pliable ball of dough that's firm, yet springy when pressed.

4   Wrap the ball of dough in plastic wrap, and rest at room temperature for 20 minutes. Meanwhile, prepare the pasta machine or dust a rolling pin and work surface with flour.

5   Using your fingers, press the dough into a rectangle. Follow the instructions that came with your pasta machine, rolling the dough until it's thin but no longer opaque. Or use a rolling pin to roll the dough into a large rectangle, turning it a quarter-turn clockwise with each roll and flipping it over several times. Dust the board with flour frequently to prevent sticking.

6   Cut the pasta sheets into your desired shape, or fill, and cook in boiling, well-salted water for about 3 minutes or until tender. Serve immediately with your favorite sauce.

2 tbsp extra-virgin olive oil

1 cup (240ml) warm water

1 tsp tomato paste and/or a pinch of saffron crushed in a mortar and pestle (optional)

3½ cups (450g) all-purpose flour, plus more for kneading

½ tsp sea salt

## Make it vegetarian

Replace the 1 cup (240ml) warm water with 4 eggs. Mix the eggs with the olive oil in step 1 and pour the mixture into the well in step 2.

# Pie Pastry

This easy pastry comes together quickly in the food processor. It yields a flaky, tender pie crust and works equally well for both sweet and savory recipes.

**makes** 2 crusts for a deep-dish pie   **prep** 10 min, plus 30 min chilling time   **cook** none

**1** In a food processor fitted with a metal blade, pulse the flour and salt several times to combine.

**2** Add half of the shortening cubes, pulse 5 or 6 times, and process for 5 seconds. Add remaining shortening and pulse until the mixture forms small, pea-sized pieces.

**3** Transfer the flour mixture to a large bowl. Pour a few tablespoons of ice water over the flour mix, and quickly toss with a fork to combine. Continue adding the water and tossing until the mixture just comes together and then use the heel of your hand to press the dough against the sides of the bowl to form a moist, cohesive ball.

**4** Separate the dough into two equal pieces, wrap in plastic wrap and use your hands to flatten each piece into a 5in (12cm) disk.

**5** Chill the dough for 30 minutes and proceed as directed in your recipe.

3 cups (375g) all-purpose, unbleached flour

1½ tsp sea salt

12 tbsp nonhydrogenated organic shortening, partially frozen, cut into small cubes (or solid coconut oil)

½–⅔ cup (120–150ml) ice water

### Make it vegetarian

Instead of shortening or coconut oil, simply use butter.

# Nut Milk

Once you've tasted homemade nut milk, you'll never go back to store-bought.

**serves** 4   **prep** 5 min, plus overnight soaking time   **cook** none

1  Soak almonds in cold water overnight.

2  Discard the soaking water, rinse the nuts well, and drain.

3  In a high-speed blender, process the nuts along with the filtered water, Medjool dates, vanilla extract, and cinnamon until smooth.

4  Using a nut milk bag or muslin bag, strain the solids from the milk into a clean glass jar.

5  Refrigerate the milk for up to 4 days. Shake well before using.

1 cup (140g) raw almonds, hazelnuts, or cashews

4 cups (960ml) filtered water

2 or 3 pitted Medjool dates

1 tsp vanilla extract

½ tsp ground cinnamon

**Why not try ...**

For Chocolate Nut Milk, add a scant 1oz (25g) raw cacao and 1 tbsp agave nectar to the blender with the other ingredients.

# Nut Butter

When properly soaked, dried nuts are easy to turn into delicious nut butter. Far better than anything from the supermarket, this nut butter is packed with healthy fat, protein, and energy.

**makes** about 30 servings of 2 tbsp   **prep** 10 min, plus overnight soaking time   **cook** none

1  Soak nuts in cold water overnight.

2  Discard the soaking water, rinse the nuts well and drain. In a food processor, pulse the nuts until they resemble flour.

3  Add the coconut oil and sea salt, and process, stopping to scrape down the sides of the bowl as needed, until the nut butter has reached your desired consistency.

4  Transfer the nut butter to a glass jar, seal tightly, and store in the fridge for up to 6 months.

4 cups (500g) raw nuts

4 tbsp coconut oil, melted

⅛ tsp sea salt

# Nut Cheese

If you're cutting back on dairy, nut cheese—which can be spreadable or hard in texture—is a tasty substitute.

**makes** about 9oz (250g)   **prep** 15 min, plus overnight soaking time   **cook** none

1  Soak nuts in cold water with 1 tsp of sea salt overnight.

2  Discard the soaking water, rinse the nuts well and drain. In a high-speed blender, process the nuts, coconut oil, lemon juice, garlic, and remaining ⅛ tsp sea salt for 5-7 minutes, or until smooth.

3  Transfer the mixture to a nut milk bag or a colander lined with cheesecloth, press down on the solids or squeeze to remove the excess liquid, and form the cheese into a ball.

4  Serve immediately, for a creamier cheese. For a harder cheese, chill in the fridge for 24 hours before serving.

1 cup (150g) raw cashews or almonds

1⅛ tsp sea salt

¾ cup (180ml) water

2 tbsp coconut oil, melted

3 tsp lemon juice

1 clove garlic

# Yogurt

Tangy, silky yogurt is easy to make and much healthier than store-bought versions. Add soaked and dried nuts or unsweetened coconut flakes, and season with cinnamon and nutmeg for a nutritious snack.

**serves** 8   **prep** 2 min   **cook** 24 hr

1   In a medium saucepan over low heat, heat the milk for about 10 minutes, or until it reaches 175°F (80°C). Use a thermometer. If you're using raw milk, heat it to 100°F (40°C).

2   Remove from the heat, and allow the milk to cool for about 10 minutes, or until it reaches 100°F (40°C).

3   Place the commercial yogurt in a 1-quart (1-liter) glass jar with a tight-fitting lid, and fill the jar with warm milk, leaving 1in (2.5cm) space at the top.

4   Place the jar in a yogurt maker or a dehydrator set to 100°F (40°C), or in the oven with the light on for 24 hours.

5   Allow the yogurt to cool in the fridge.

4 cups (950ml) organic raw or lightly pasteurized unhomogenized whole milk

¼ cup (60ml) organic commercial yogurt

## Make it vegan

Substitute one 13.5fl oz (400ml) can of coconut milk for the organic whole milk. Shake the can vigorously before opening. Add 1 probiotic capsule to the coconut milk, and culture as directed.

# Vegan Mayonnaise

You can easily find vegan mayonnaise at the supermarket, but this simple recipe will have you making your own in no time! The soy milk helps with thickening, allowing you to replicate the smooth texture of mayonnaise.

**makes** 1 cup (250ml) **prep** 5 min **cook** none

1 Combine all the ingredients except the oil in a high-speed blender and blend on high for 1 minute.

2 Reduce the speed to low and slowly pour in the oil until the mixture begins to thicken.

3 Taste the mayonnaise and adjust accordingly. Add more oil for a creamier mayonnaise, or add more mustard, agave nectar, vinegar, or salt to taste.

½ cup (120ml) unsweetened soy milk

1 tsp apple cider vinegar

juice of ½ lemon (1 tbsp)

½ tsp agave nectar (or sweetener of your choice)

½ tsp Dijon mustard

¾ tsp salt

1 cup (250ml) grape-seed oil (or any neutral-tasting vegetable oil)

### Why not try ...

You can also try using silken tofu to make vegan mayonnaise. Replace the soy milk in this recipe with 8oz (225g) silken tofu and use only 3 tbsp grape-seed oil. Drain the tofu and transfer to a blender. Add the remaining ingredients and blend until smooth and creamy.

# Tofu

While widely considered a health food, tofu is a staple of both vegetarian and Japanese diets. You can find tofu in many different varieties: silken, soft, firm, and extra firm. Tofu is made from mature soy beans that have been dried (known as daizu), as well as nigari, which acts as a coagulant (solidifier). If you'd like fresh firm tofu to add to your flexitarian meals, simply follow these steps.

**makes** 14oz (400g)   **prep** 1 hr, plus overnight soaking time   **cook** 20 min

1 In a large bowl filled with 4¼ cups (1 liter) of water, soak the dried soy beans overnight, about 8–12 hours.

2 In a food processor, grind the soy beans and soaking water for 2 minutes, or until fine.

3 In a large pan over medium heat, bring 5 cups (1.2 liters) of water to a boil. Add the ground soy beans and stir continuously with a wooden spatula. Just before the mixture comes to a boil, reduce the heat to low and cook, stirring continuously, for 8 minutes.

4 Line a colander with cheesecloth, and place over a large pan. Strain the mixture through the cloth, and discard the solids.

5 Cook the soy milk strained into the pan over low heat, stirring continuously with a wooden spatula. When the temperature registers between 151–154°F (66–68°C), remove the pan from the heat.

6 In a small bowl filled with 6 tablespoons of lukewarm water, dissolve the nigari.

7 Add half of the nigari mixture to the soy milk, stirring with the spatula in a whirlpool pattern. While the soy milk is swirling, add the remaining nigari mixture, stirring gently afterward in a figure-eight pattern. You should notice the soy milk beginning to coagulate. Cover the pan, and leave to stand for 15 minutes.

8 Line a colander with cheesecloth (don't reuse the previous one), and set over a bowl that can support it. With a soup ladle, gently transfer the coagulated soy milk to the cloth-lined colander.

9 Fold the cloth over the coagulated soy milk, and place a weight on top. Leave to stand for 15 minutes.

10 Remove the weight and gently transfer the bowl to a sink filled with cold water to cool. Once chilled, unfold the cloth, and gently lift out the finished tofu.

11 Use the tofu immediately, or store in an airtight container with fresh, cold water in the fridge for up to 1 week.

1¼ cups (200g) dried soy beans

2 tsp nigari (found in Japanese supermarkets or health food stores)

# Béchamel Sauce

Smooth béchamel is the perfect choice when a creamy sauce is desired. A hint of onion, clove, and nutmeg adds just a bit of spice to this delicious and versatile sauce.

**makes** 2 cups (480ml)  **prep** 5 min  **cook** 10-15 min

1  Heat the grape-seed oil in a small saucepan over medium–high heat. Add the flour all at once and stir vigorously with a whisk.

2  When the flour mixture is golden and begins to smell nutty (but before it browns, about 2 minutes), add the nondairy milk, continuing to whisk vigorously to prevent lumps.

3  Add the clove-studded onion and bay leaf, reduce the heat to low, and cook, stirring frequently, for about 10 minutes or until the sauce thickens.

4  Remove from the heat, and stir in salt, pepper, and nutmeg. Taste and adjust seasonings.

5  Strain the sauce through a fine-mesh sieve to remove any solids, and use immediately.

¼ cup grape-seed oil

3 tbsp all-purpose flour

2½ cups (600ml) unflavored nondairy milk, preferably soy or rice

¼ small onion, studded with 1 whole clove

1 bay leaf

¼ tsp sea salt

pinch freshly ground black pepper

pinch freshly grated nutmeg

### Make it vegetarian

If you'd like a dairy béchamel sauce, replace the grape-seed oil with butter and the nondairy milk with cow's milk.

# Mushroom Gravy

This rich, brown, flavorful gravy never disappoints. Using a mushroom stock (see page 30) and taking time to cook the roux without burning it are the secrets to this great gravy.

**makes** 4 cups (960ml)  **prep** 10 min  **cook** 30 min

1  Heat 3 tablespoons of the grape-seed oil in a medium frying pan over medium–high heat until it shimmers (but before it begins to smoke). Add the shallots and cook, stirring occasionally, for about 5 minutes or until softened.

2  Add the garlic and chestnut and shiitake mushrooms and cook, stirring often, for 10 minutes or until the mushrooms have released their liquid.

3  Add the mushroom stock and tamari, reduce the heat to medium, and cook, stirring occasionally, while you make the roux.

4  In a small pan over medium heat, heat the remaining 2 tablespoons of grape-seed oil. Whisk in the flour and cook, stirring frequently, for about 10 minutes or until the mixture is a rich brown color.

5  Whisk the roux into the mushroom mixture, and cook for a further 5–10 minutes or until the gravy is as thick as you like it. Stir in bourbon (if using) and black pepper, and serve immediately. This gravy will keep in a tightly sealed container in the fridge for 3 days.

- 5 tbsp grape-seed oil
- 2 medium shallots, finely chopped
- 1 clove garlic, smashed and finely chopped
- 3 cups (225g) thinly sliced cremini (baby bella) mushrooms
- 2⅓ cups (225g) thinly sliced shiitake mushrooms
- 4 cups (960ml) Mushroom Stock (see page 30)
- 1 tbsp salt-reduced tamari or soy sauce
- 3 tbsp all-purpose flour
- 1 tbsp bourbon (optional)
- ½ tsp freshly ground black pepper

# Tomato Sauce

This simple, fresh-tasting tomato sauce comes together in minutes. Use the best-quality canned tomatoes you can find for this quick and easy sauce that's perfect with pasta or as a base for soup.

**makes** 3½ cups (840ml)  **prep** 5 min  **cook** 15 min

1  Heat the olive oil in a large saucepan over medium–high heat. When the oil is shimmering (but before it begins to smoke), add the garlic and salt. Cook, stirring, for 30 seconds, to allow the garlic to release its fragrance without browning.

2  Add the tomatoes with their juice and the white wine to the pan, and cook for 5 minutes.

3  Using a potato masher or a large fork, crush the tomatoes. Reduce the heat to medium and cook, stirring occasionally, for a further 10 minutes.

4  Stir in the basil and pepper, and remove from the heat.

5  Use immediately, or pour into freezer-safe containers with 1in (2.5cm) headspace and freeze for up to 3 months.

- 2 tbsp extra-virgin olive oil
- 2 cloves garlic, peeled, smashed and finely chopped
- ½ tsp sea salt
- 1 (28oz/800g) can peeled tomatoes, with juice
- ½ cup dry white wine
- 4 leaves fresh basil, torn
- ¼ tsp freshly ground black pepper

# Breakfast

Break up your usual breakfast routine with these delicious, modern recipes. Some are perfect for leisurely brunches, while others can be made ahead for a no-fuss midweek breakfast.

# Curried Mung Bean Avocado Toast

Sprouts and mung beans elevate avocado toast to the next level of tasty. The hint of curry flavor adds extra depth to the creamy, smooth avocado.

**makes** 3   **prep** 10 min   **cook** 4 min

1   In a frying pan over medium-low heat, toast the bread for 2 minutes on each side, or until brown and crisp. Remove from the frying pan and let cool slightly.

2   Cut the avocado in half and remove the pit. Scoop the flesh from one half and add to a medium mixing bowl. Mash the avocado half with a potato masher.

3   Stir in the mung beans, curry powder, and turmeric. Season with salt and pepper to taste. Spread the avocado mixture evenly over the slices of toast.

4   Remove the flesh from the remaining avocado half and slice thinly. Arrange equal amounts on each slice of toast.

5   Place on serving plates and sprinkle with the bean sprouts and chives. Serve immediately.

3 slices of sourdough or whole wheat bread

1 ripe avocado

1 cup (175g) cooked mung beans

½ tsp curry powder

pinch of turmeric

salt and freshly ground black pepper

¾ cup (45g) sprouted mung beans (bean sprouts)

3 tbsp chopped chives

## Make it with meat

Crumble 2 slices of cooked, crispy bacon into the avocado–mung bean mixture.

# Lentil Cream Cheese Tartines

Flavored cream cheese is very easy to make at home. Adding lentils, chives, and lemon zest provides texture and some extra protein to this simple breakfast dish.

**makes** 6   **prep** 5 min   **cook** 25 min

1 Preheat the oven to 300°F (150°C). Arrange the slices of bread on a baking sheet. Toast for 5 minutes, turn over, and toast for another 5 minutes until crisp and golden.

2 Meanwhile, to make the cream cheese spread, in a food processor blend the cream cheese, lentils, chives, and lemon zest until thoroughly combined. Season with salt and pepper to taste. Spread the mixture evenly over the slices of toast.

3 In a nonstick frying pan, heat 1 teaspoon of oil over medium-low heat until shimmering. Crack 2 eggs into the frying pan and cook for 2–3 minutes until the whites are set but the yolks are runny. Place each egg atop a slice of toast then repeat with the remaining 4 eggs. Top each tartine with watercress and serve immediately.

6 slices whole wheat bread

8oz (225g) cream cheese, softened

¾ cup (100g) cooked brown lentils

2 tbsp chopped chives

zest of 1 lemon

salt and freshly ground black pepper

3 tsp olive oil

6 large eggs

2 cups (115g) watercress

### Make it vegan

Use a nut cheese (see page 37) instead of cream cheese and omit the eggs from this recipe.

### Make it with fish

Top each tartine with 1oz (30g) thinly sliced smoked salmon.

# Roasted Tomato and Chickpea Frittata

Frittatas are a wonderful way to feed a crowd for breakfast or brunch. Chickpeas add an unexpected twist and extra body to this morning classic.

**serves** 10   **prep** 15 min   **cook** 30 min

**1** Preheat the oven to 400°F (200°C). On a baking tray, toss the tomatoes, garlic, and thyme in the oil. Spread in an even layer and roast for 10 minutes. Discard the thyme. Let cool slightly.

**2** Meanwhile, in a large mixing bowl whisk together the eggs, heavy cream, and chives. Season with salt and pepper.

**3** Heat a 10in (25cm) cast-iron or ovenproof frying pan over medium heat. Transfer the tomatoes to the frying pan. Add the spinach and cook for 1–2 minutes until the spinach slightly wilts. Add the chickpeas and stir to combine. Spread the mixture evenly across the frying pan.

**4** Pour the egg mixture over the tomatoes, spinach, and chickpeas. Cook uncovered for 2–3 minutes, until the edges of the egg begin to set. Transfer the frying pan to the oven and cook uncovered for an additional 8–10 minutes, until the edges are firm but the center is still slightly springy. Serve immediately.

1lb (450g) grape tomatoes

1 clove garlic, finely chopped

2 sprigs of thyme

1 tbsp olive oil

10 large eggs

2 tbsp heavy cream

2 tsp chopped chives

salt and freshly ground black pepper

3 cups (85g) baby spinach

2 cups (350g) cooked chickpeas

## Why not try ...

For a creamy tang, sprinkle 4oz (115g) goat cheese over the egg mixture before baking.

### Make it with meat

Add 5oz (140g) finely diced cooked ham or chicken sausage to the frying pan with the chickpeas in step 3.

# Spinach and Artichoke Quiche

This tasty quiche uses amaranth flour for a delicious crust and is ideal for a healthy and filling brunch. For best results, use artichokes that have been preserved in oil instead of those canned in water or brine.

**serves** 6   **prep** 20 min   **cook** 50 min

1   Preheat the oven to 400°F (200°C). Grease a 9in (22cm) loose-bottomed flan pan and set aside. For the pastry, add amaranth flour, tapioca flour, almonds, and salt to a large bowl and mix well until combined. In a small bowl, whisk together the oil and water. Make a well in the center of the dry ingredients and pour the oil mixture in. Bring together to form a light and sticky dough, adding more water, a little at a time, if needed.

2   Roll out the dough between two sheets of plastic wrap and use to line the prepared pan, making sure it forms a good side to the case. Prick the bottom of the pastry with a fork. Place in the oven and blind bake for about 10 minutes. Then remove from the heat and set aside. Reduce the oven temperature to 350°F (180°C).

3   For the filling, heat the oil in a large saucepan over medium heat. Add the garlic and onions and cook for about 3–5 minutes or until the onions are translucent. Then add the spinach and cook for a further 2–3 minutes or until it has wilted. Remove from the heat and set aside.

4   For the custard, place the eggs, egg yolks, and milk in a large bowl. Season with ¼ teaspoon salt and a good grinding of pepper. Whisk until well combined. Spoon the onion and spinach mixture into the pastry case, making sure it covers the bottom. Spread out the artichoke hearts on top in a single layer and pour over the custard. Crumble the goat cheese and sprinkle over the custard.

5   Bake the quiche in the oven for about 40 minutes or until the custard has set and the top is golden. Remove from the heat and leave to cool slightly before cutting into wedges to serve. This quiche can be served warm or at room temperature.

### For the pastry

½ cup (70g) amaranth flour

⅓ cup (45g) tapioca flour or cornstarch

¼ cup (30g) ground almonds

¼ tsp salt

3 tbsp sunflower oil

3 tbsp water

### For the filling

1 tbsp olive oil

1 clove garlic, crushed

¾ cup (110g) finely chopped onion

4½ cups (140g) spinach

4–5 artichoke hearts, drained and roughly chopped

2oz (60g) goat cheese

### For the custard

2 large eggs

2 egg yolks

1 cup (250ml) whole milk

salt and freshly ground black pepper

# Black Bean Breakfast Tostadas

These crunchy fried tortillas are topped with creamy scrambled eggs and spicy, savory black beans for an irresistible Mexican-style breakfast.

**serves** 4   **prep** 15 min   **cook** 20 min

1   Preheat the oven to 325°F (170°C). In a medium frying pan, heat the oil over medium-low heat. Add the onion and cook for 5 minutes, or until translucent. Add the jalapeño and garlic and cook for an additional 2–3 minutes.

2   Add the black beans, cumin, and chipotle chili powder and stir to coat. Add the stock, bring to a boil, then reduce to a simmer and cook for 5 minutes, or until the liquid reduces. Season with salt and pepper to taste.

3   Meanwhile, arrange the tostada shells on a baking tray in an even layer, with their edges slightly overlapping. Bake for 2–3 minutes until warmed through.

4   In a small mixing bowl, whisk together the eggs and heavy cream. In a nonstick frying pan, over medium-low heat, scramble the eggs to the desired consistency.

5   To assemble, spread equal amounts of the black bean mixture on the tostada shells. Top with equal amounts of scrambled eggs. Sprinkle a quarter of the Cotija on each tostada, then garnish with cilantro and hot sauce. Serve immediately.

1 tbsp olive oil

1 small onion, finely diced

1 jalapeño, seeded and finely diced

1 clove garlic, finely chopped

2 cups (350g) cooked black beans

1 tbsp ground cumin

1 tsp chipotle chili powder

½ cup (120ml) vegetable stock

salt and freshly ground black pepper

4 corn tostada shells

4 large eggs

1½ tsp heavy cream

4oz (115g) Cotija cheese

sprigs of cilantro, to garnish

hot sauce, to garnish

### Why not try ...

For a boost of healthy fats, top each tostada with wedges of sliced avocado.

### Make it vegan

Instead of eggs and heavy cream, scramble 8oz (225g) firm tofu with salt and pepper. For the feta, use a nut cheese (see page 37).

### Make it with meat

Crumble 1 slice of crispy bacon over the beans as you assemble the tostadas.

# Asparagus and Green Lentils with Poached Egg

This impressive-looking brunch dish couldn't be easier to prepare. The yolk from the poached egg makes a luxurious sauce for the roasted asparagus and lentils.

**serves** 4  **prep** 10 min  **cook** 15 min

1 Preheat the oven to 350°F (180°C). Toss the asparagus with 1 tablespoon of oil. Arrange on a baking tray in a single layer and season with salt and pepper. Roast for 10 minutes, or until tender.

2 Meanwhile, to make the dressing, in a medium bowl combine the red wine vinegar, Dijon mustard, thyme, and remaining 1 tablespoon of oil. Whisk until emulsified. Add the lentils and stir to combine. Set aside and let the lentils absorb the dressing.

3 To poach the eggs, fill a large saucepan with water, about 1½in (4cm) deep. Bring to a boil then reduce to a simmer. Add the white vinegar. One at a time, crack each egg into a ramekin and gently tip it into the water. Cook for 3 minutes. Drain and place on a plate lined with kitchen paper.

4 To serve, divide the asparagus among 4 plates and top each with the lentils. Place 1 poached egg atop the lentils. Season with pepper and serve immediately.

1lb (450g) fine asparagus, woody ends trimmed

2 tbsp olive oil

salt and freshly ground black pepper

2½ tbsp red wine vinegar

1 tbsp Dijon mustard

¼ tsp chopped thyme

1⅓ cups (400g) cooked green lentils

⅛ tsp of white vinegar

4 large eggs

### Make it with meat

Add 1 slice of prosciutto or a slice of crispy bacon to each plate.

# Spiced Apple and Mung Bean Muffins

Mung beans pureed with apple sauce make for one of the moistest muffins you'll ever taste and provide protein and fiber for a filling on-the-go breakfast.

**serves** 12   **prep** 35 min   **cook** 20 min

1  Preheat the oven to 350°F (175°C). In a food processor, combine the applesauce, mung beans, and agave. Puree until smooth.

2  In a large mixing bowl, whisk together the whole wheat flour, all-purpose flour, baking powder, cinnamon, and nutmeg.

3  In a medium mixing bowl, add the egg, brown sugar, almond milk, and bean mixture. Whisk until thoroughly combined.

4  Add the bean mixture to the flour mixture and stir until no streaks of dry ingredients remain. Gently fold in the diced apples until combined.

5  Line a 12-cup muffin tin with paper liners. Place 2 tablespoons of the mixture into each cup. Sprinkle the top of each muffin with 1 teaspoon of oats. Bake for 20–25 minutes until set, and a skewer inserted into the center of the muffin comes out clean. Let rest for an hour before serving. Store in an airtight container for up to 2 days.

⅔ cup (150g) unsweetened applesauce

½ cup (85g) cooked mung beans

2 tbsp agave nectar

¾ cup (100g) whole wheat flour

¾ cup (100g) all-purpose flour

2 tsp baking powder

1 tsp cinnamon

pinch of ground nutmeg

1 large egg

½ cup (100g) packed light brown sugar

⅓ cup (80ml) unsweetened almond milk

1 medium Granny Smith apple, peeled, cored, and finely diced

¼ cup (20g) old fashioned oats

## Make it vegan

Substitute half a mashed banana for the egg.

# Tropical Smoothie Bowl

The bright flavors of pineapple and mango are complemented by velvety white beans and banana in these beautiful, protein-rich bowls.

**makes** 2   **prep** 10 min   **cook** none

1 Withhold a bit of mango, pineapple, and banana for the garnish. In a blender, add the remainder of the fruit, along with the honey, yogurt, and cannellini beans. Puree until completely smooth.

2 Divide the smoothie between 2 bowls, and garnish with toasted coconut, chia seeds, and the reserved mango, pineapple, and banana. Serve immediately.

1 cup (175g) diced mango

1 cup (200g) diced pineapple

1 banana, sliced

1 tbsp honey or agave nectar

¾ cup (200g) yogurt (see page 38)

½ cup (85g) cooked cannellini beans

¼ cup (15g) toasted coconut, to garnish

2 tsp chia seeds, to garnish

### Make it vegan

Use a vegan yogurt alternative, such as coconut yogurt (see page 38), rather than dairy yogurt.

# Whole Wheat Pancakes with Apple and Cinnamon

Whole wheat flour gives these pancakes a rustic texture and nutty flavor, while apple adds sweetness and moisture.

**makes** 8 **prep** 15 min **cook** 6 min

1 In a large bowl, whisk together the whole wheat flour, baking powder, sugar, cinnamon, and salt. In a small bowl, beat together the egg and milk.

2 Make a well in the center of the dry ingredients and pour in the milk mixture, whisking to combine. Once it is completely mixed, add the cooled, melted butter and whisk again. Gently fold in the grated apple.

3 In a large nonstick frying pan, melt a little butter over medium heat. Spoon small amounts of batter into the hot pan, to create pancakes about 4in (10cm) across. Use the back of the spoon to smooth over the tops of the pancakes.

4 Cook for 3 minutes over medium-low heat, until they look set around the edges. Carefully turn over and cook for another 2–3 minutes. Serve immediately with maple syrup and apple slices pan-fried in butter and finished with lemon juice (if using).

1 cup (150g) whole wheat flour

1 tsp baking powder

1 tbsp sugar

½ tsp ground cinnamon

⅛ tsp fine sea salt

1 large egg

⅔ cup (160ml) whole milk

1 tbsp unsalted butter, melted and cooled, plus extra for frying

1 apple, peeled, cored, and finely grated

**To serve**

maple syrup

a few apple slices (optional)

lemon juice (optional)

### Make it vegan

Mix together 1 tbsp chia seeds with 3 tbsp warm water, let it sit for 15 minutes, and use this instead of the egg in step 1. Instead of dairy milk and butter, use soy milk and margarine.

# Wheat Berry Bircher Muesli Pots

Perfect for spring or summer, these bircher muesli pots replace the traditional oats with wheat berries that add a delicious nutty flavor and texture.

**serves** 4   **prep** 25 min, plus overnight soaking and cooling   **cook** 30 min

1  Place the wheat berries in a large bowl, cover with water, and leave to soak overnight or for up to 8 hours. Then drain well, rinse under running water, and drain again.

2  Place the wheat berries in a large saucepan, cover with plenty of water, and bring to a boil. Then reduce the heat to a simmer, cover, and cook for 30 minutes or until the wheat berries are tender. Remove from the heat, drain any remaining water, and leave to cool completely.

3  Meanwhile, wash the blueberries and place them in a separate bowl. Wash the strawberries and cut them into thin slices. Add them to the blueberries and toss to mix. Once cooled, place the wheat berries, yogurt, sunflower seeds, and honey in a large bowl. Mix until well combined.

4  Divide half the wheat berry and yogurt mixture equally between 4 serving bowls, glasses, or jars. Top with a layer of half the strawberries and blueberries. Repeat the process adding one more layer of yogurt and fruit. Sprinkle over some sunflower seeds and add a drizzle of honey before serving.

⅔ cup (120g) uncooked wheat berries

1¾ cups (250g) blueberries

1¾ cups (250g) strawberries, hulled

1⅔ cups (400g) yogurt (see page 38)

¼ cup sunflower seeds, plus extra to serve

¼ cup honey, plus extra to serve

## Why not try ...

Try adding raspberries and blackberries in place of the blueberries and strawberries.

### Make it vegan

Substitute the dairy yogurt for a vegan alternative, such as coconut yogurt (see page 38), and use maple syrup or agave nectar instead of honey.

# Snacks, Dips, and Light Bites

Sometimes you need a little something small to tide you over between main meals. These nutritious small bites are perfect for snacking, enjoying as appetizers, or serving as finger food to guests.

# Raw Energy Bars

Mix and match the dried fruits and seeds in these healthy energy bars as you like, but keep the quantities the same.

**makes** 16  **prep** 10 min, plus 4 hr chilling time  **cook** none

1 Put the dates and prunes in a heatproof bowl and cover with hot water. Leave to soak for 5 minutes. Put the hazelnuts in a food processor and pulse until they are broken up into pieces.

2 Drain the dates and prunes and loosely squeeze them dry, leaving them still damp. Place them in the food processor with the hazelnuts and add all the remaining ingredients.

3 Process the mixture until it is well combined, the nuts and seeds are in small pieces, and the mixture begins to form a ball. It will be very stiff, so you may need to scrape down the sides of the bowl and break it up occasionally with a spatula.

4 Turn out the mixture into a 9in (23cm) square baking pan, and use dampened hands to push it into an even layer. Use the back of a large metal spoon, dampened, to even out the surface of the mixture, then cover, and chill for at least 3-4 hours.

5 Turn out the mixture onto a board and cut into 16 equal-sized pieces. Wrap individually in parchment paper and store in an airtight container in the refrigerator until needed.

1 cup (150g) roughly chopped pitted Medjool dates

½ cup (100g) roughly chopped pitted prunes

½ cup (60g) raw hazelnuts

½ cup (60g) buckwheat flour

½ cup (50g) raw sliced almonds

½ cup (30g) unsweetened flaked coconut

⅓ cup (60g) roughly chopped dried cherries

¼ cup (30g) sprouted pumpkin seeds

¼ cup (30g) sprouted sunflower seeds

2 tbsp raw cacao powder

# Cranberry, Orange, and Chocolate Quinoa Bars

The perfect handy snack, these sweet, chewy, and wholesome bars feel like a treat, but pack a big nutritional punch and will keep you full for hours.

**makes** 12 bars   **prep** 20 min, plus cooling   **cook** 5 min

1 Place the almonds, quinoa flakes, sunflower seeds, chia seeds, dried cranberries, puffed rice cereal, chocolate chips, and orange zest in a bowl. Mix well with a wooden spoon and set aside. Grease and line a 8×10in (20×25cm) baking pan with wax paper.

2 Heat the oil, honey, and sugar in a saucepan over a medium heat. Cook, stirring occasionally, for about 5 minutes or until the sugar has melted and the mixture is bubbling. Set aside to cool for about 2 minutes.

3 Pour the cooled honey mixture into the dry ingredients. Mix using a wooden spoon until well incorporated, making sure the chocolate chips have melted and are evenly combined. Spoon the mixture into the prepared baking pan. Press down firmly with the back of a wooden spoon to make a roughly even layer.

4 Place the baking pan in the fridge for at least 4 hours, to allow the mixture to cool and harden. Remove from the fridge, turn out onto a cutting board, and cut into bars. These can be stored in an airtight container in the fridge for up to 5 days.

1 cup (120g) almonds, roughly chopped

3 cups (120g) quinoa flakes

¾ cup (35g) sunflower seeds

¾ cup (35g) chia seeds

⅔ cup (100g) dried cranberries

6 cups (125g) puffed rice cereal

1¾oz (50g) dark chocolate chips

grated zest of 2 large oranges

⅓ cup (85ml) coconut oil

½ cup (120ml) honey

¼ cup (35g) unpacked light brown sugar

## Why not try ...

Add walnuts instead of the almonds, pumpkin seeds instead of sunflower seeds, and raisins or chopped dates instead of the cranberries. In each case, use the same amount of the substitute ingredient as recommended in the recipe.

### Make it vegan

Buy vegan dark chocolate chips, or replace the chocolate chips with extra dried cranberries. Instead of honey, use rice malt syrup.

# Spicy Carrot Hummus

Harissa is a natural match for the sweetness of carrots and the tang of tahini in this hummus. Serve with crisp vegetables or seeded crackers.

**serves** 6   **prep** 20 min   **cook** 30 min

1   Preheat the oven to 350°F (180°C). Peel the carrots and cut into 1in (3cm) chunks. Toss with 1 tablespoon of oil and arrange in a single layer on a baking tray. Roast for 25–30 minutes, until caramelized and tender. Remove from the oven and leave to cool.

2   In a food processor, combine the chickpeas and water and process briefly to combine. Add the tahini, lime juice, harissa, and roasted carrots. With the processor running on low, drizzle in the oil. Season with salt and pepper to taste, then pulse a few more times to combine. Serve immediately.

¾ lb (350g) carrots, ends trimmed, around 7-8 carrots

¼ cup (60ml) olive oil, plus 1 tbsp for roasting

2 cups (350g) cooked chickpeas, peeled

1 tbsp water

1½ tbsp tahini

juice of 1 large lime

1 tbsp harissa paste

salt and freshly ground black pepper

## Why not try ...

Replace the chickpeas with an equal amount of cooked cannellini or navy beans.

# White Bean Butter with Radishes

Radishes with butter and salt are a classic French snack. Here, the butter is browned and blended with white beans to make a luxurious and creamy dip.

**serves** 4  **prep** 5 min  **cook** 10 min

1 In a small saucepan, melt the butter over a low heat. Cook until the butter takes on a light brown color and nutty aroma, then remove from the heat.

2 In a food processor, combine the butter, cannellini beans, and garlic. Blend on high until smooth, adding water as needed to reach the desired consistency.

3 Transfer the dip to a small bowl and serve alongside radishes and a small dish of sea salt.

2 tbsp unsalted butter

1 cup (175g) cooked cannellini beans

1 clove garlic

1 tsp water (optional)

1 bunch radishes, washed, and tops removed

flaky sea salt

### Make it vegan

Omit the butter for a more traditional white bean dip.

# Adzuki Bean Summer Rolls with Peanut Sauce

Spiralized jicama replaces traditional rice noodles in these summer rolls. Adzuki beans complement the sweet mango and creamy avocado.

**makes** 16   **prep** 1 hr   **cook** none

1   To make the peanut sauce, in a small bowl whisk together the peanut butter, lime juice, vinegar, water, and sriracha until smooth. Set aside until ready to serve.

2   Cut the jicama into even chunks. Adjust a spiralizer to the thinnest blade and spiralize the jicama. Set out the jicama, mint, mango, onion, avocado, adzuki beans, and cilantro on your worktop to prepare for filling the rolls.

3   Pour warm water into a shallow flan or pie dish. One at a time, submerge the rice paper wrappers into warm water for 30 seconds, or until pliable without tearing. Remove from the water and place onto a clean, flat, nonstick surface, such as a plastic or ceramic cutting board.

4   Arrange the desired amount of mint leaves, mango, red onion, avocado, adzuki beans, cilantro, and spiralized jicama in the center of the wrapper, working quickly so that it doesn't dry out. Do not overstuff the wrapper, or it will tear. Fold the bottom edge over the filling, and press to seal. Then fold the sides toward the center, tucking in the filling. Roll gently and seal firmly.

5   Repeat to use all the remaining ingredients. Serve with peanut sauce on the side. Store in the fridge for 2-3 days, individually wrapped so they do not stick together.

½ cup (125g) creamy peanut butter

juice of 1 lime

1 tbsp rice wine vinegar

⅓ cup (80ml) water

½ tsp sriracha

1 small jicama, peeled (if you can't find jicama, try using water chestnuts or Jerusalem artichokes)

1oz (25g) mint leaves

1 mango, peeled, stoned, and cut into ½in (1cm) slices

1 small red onion, julienned

1 avocado, pitted and cut into ¼in (5mm) slices

1½ cups (325g) cooked adzuki beans

2 cups (60g) cilantro

1 package of spring roll rice paper wrappers

## Make it with fish

Horizontally slice 1 cooked large shrimp for each roll, and place atop the mint during assembly.

# Shirataki and Shrimp Summer Rolls

These light and tasty rolls are stuffed with shirataki noodles, shrimp, and fresh herbs, but they can take a variety of fillings. Use vibrant, crisp vegetables and mix and match as you prefer.

**makes** 8 rolls   **prep** 30 min   **cook** none

1  To make the dipping sauce: in a small saucepan, heat the sugar and water over medium heat, whisking frequently, until the sugar has dissolved. Remove from the heat and leave to cool. Then add the remaining ingredients and whisk to combine.

2  Fill a large bowl with warm water. Fully submerge 1 rice paper wrapper for 10 to 15 seconds until it just starts to soften. Shake any excess water from it, and lay it flat on a clean work surface.

3  Take 2 shrimp halves and lay them pink-side down along the center of the wrapper. Top the shrimp with a few leaves of mint, basil, and cilantro. Then add a little of the shirataki noodles, a few julienned carrots and spring onions, and a few pea shoots, leaving the edges of the wrapper free. Finish with 2 more shrimp halves, pink-side up.

4  The wrapper should be fully softened and pliable by now, but not too delicate. Wrap the side nearest to you up over the filling, tuck the outside edges up over the filling, and roll the wrapper away from you, tucking as you go, to fully encase the filling. Place on a plate, cover with damp paper towel, and refrigerate. Repeat steps 2 to 4 to make all 8 rolls, continuing to chill them as you go.

5  After assembling all 8 rolls, serve immediately with the dipping sauce on the side.

8 (6in/15cm) rice paper wrappers

16 large, cooked shrimp, halved horizontally

small handful of mint

small handful of Thai basil

small handful of cilantro

2 (8oz/200g) packages shirataki noodles, drained, rinsed, and dried

1 large carrot, julienned

4 spring onions, julienned

small handful of pea shoots

**for the dipping sauce**

2 tbsp sugar

2 tbsp water

1½ tbsp fish sauce

1 tbsp rice wine vinegar

juice of 1 lime

½ clove garlic, crushed

pinch of red pepper flakes

### Make it vegan

These summer rolls will taste just as great without shrimp. But you could also add extra vegetables or slices of firm tofu if you wish.

# Spiralized Beet and Onion Bhajis

These crispy Indian fritters can be eaten as an appetizer or snack. The spiralized beet adds a vivid pink color.

**serves** 12   **prep** 15 min   **cook** 15 min

1 In a large fire-resistant casserole or heavy-bottomed saucepan, heat the canola oil over medium-low heat. Measuring with a deep frying thermometer, bring to 350°F (180°C).

2 Meanwhile, to make the cucumber sauce, in a small bowl stir together the yogurt and cucumber.

3 Adjust a spiralizer to the thinnest blade and spiralize the onion and beet. With kitchen scissors, trim into 1in (3cm) lengths.

4 In a large mixing bowl, whisk together the turmeric, salt, chickpea flour, and water. Gradually add water to reach the consistency of pancake batter. Add the beet and onion and toss to combine.

5 With your hands, gather 2 tablespoons of the bhaji mixture and carefully drop into the oil. Fry for 4 minutes, or until golden and crispy, rotating once. Place on a plate lined with paper towel and repeat with the remaining batter. Serve immediately with the cucumber sauce.

4 cups (1 liter) canola oil
1 cup (200g) plain Greek yogurt
1 small cucumber, peeled and grated
1 large onion, peeled
1 large beet, peeled
pinch of turmeric
½ tsp salt
¾ cup (75g) chickpea flour
½ cup (120ml) water

## Make it vegan

Replace the Greek yogurt in the sauce with the same quantity of coconut milk yogurt (see page 38).

# Quinoa and Moth Bean Dolmades

Distinctive dill and mint combine with the textures of currants and pine nuts in these stuffed vine leaves, whose flavors develop over time for a delicious make-ahead lunch.

**makes** 24　**prep** 30 min　**cook** 1 hr

1　Preheat the oven to 350°F (180°C). Lightly grease a 9×12in (23×30cm) glass or ceramic baking dish. Fill a large bowl with warm water. Soak the vine leaves for 2–3 minutes until pliable. Drain in a colander. Cover the colander with a wet towel, so they remain moist during assembly.

2　To make the filling, in a large mixing bowl combine the quinoa, mint, dill, parsley, currants, pine nuts, 1 tablespoon of oil, 1 tablespoon of lemon juice, and the cooked moth beans (or lentils). Season with salt and pepper.

3　To assemble the dolmades, place one vine leaf on a clean, flat work surface, vein-side up, and cut off the stem. Place 1 heaped tablespoon of filling in the center, toward the bottom of the leaf. Fold the sides over the filling and roll tightly from stem to tip. Place seam-side down in the baking dish. Repeat with the remaining leaves, arranging snugly.

4　Pour the stock over the dolmades and drizzle over the remaining 1 tablespoon of oil and 2 tablespoons of lemon juice.

5　Cover the baking dish with foil and bake for 20–30 minutes until all the liquid has absorbed and the dolmades are moist and steaming. Serve immediately or leave to cool and store in an airtight container in the fridge for up to 2 days.

8oz (225g) jar of vine leaves, minimum 24 leaves

1 cup (140g) cooked quinoa

1½ tbsp chopped mint

1½ tbsp chopped dill

1½ tbsp chopped flat-leaf parsley

¼ cup (45g) dried currants

¼ cup (30g) toasted pine nuts

2 tbsp olive oil

3 tbsp lemon juice

1 cup (300g) cooked moth beans, or black lentils

salt and freshly ground black pepper

1 cup (240ml) vegetable stock

## Why not try ...

For a tangier bite, sprinkle 1½oz (45g) of finely crumbled feta cheese or nut cheese into the quinoa filling before rolling the dolmades.

### Make it with meat

Stir in 1½oz (45g) cooked ground lamb or beef with the quinoa filling.

# Masala Chickpea Nachos

This hybrid recipe combines the warm spices of Indian cuisine with the cheesy crunch of Tex-Mex nachos.

**serves** 6   **prep** 40 mins   **cook** 20 mins

1  To make the cilantro-mint sauce, in a blender combine two-thirds of the cilantro with the mint, lemon juice, ginger, and water. Puree until smooth. Season with salt and pepper. Transfer to an airtight container and set aside.

2  Preheat the oven to 400°F (200°C). Line a baking sheet with foil. Toss the chickpeas with the curry powder, garam masala, and oil. Spread in an even layer on the baking sheet and bake for 10 minutes, or until just crispy and warmed through. Transfer to a bowl and wipe the baking sheet.

3  Break each popadam into quarters and arrange in a single layer on the baking sheet. Sprinkle half the mozzarella over the popadams and top with the chickpea mixture. Then top with the remaining mozzarella and bake for 10–12 minutes, until the mozzarella melts and the popadams are lightly brown.

4  Meanwhile, in a small saucepan, heat the mango chutney with 1 tablespoon of water. Cook for 2–3 minutes until thin and warmed through.

5  To finish the assembly, sprinkle the onion over the melted cheese and drizzle mango chutney sauce over the top. Dollop the cilantro-mint sauce across the nachos. Chop the remaining cilantro and sprinkle over the nachos. Garnish with lime wedges and serve immediately, directly from the baking sheet.

3 cups (125g) cilantro

1 cup (30g) mint

2 tbsp lemon juice

¼ tsp ground ginger

⅓ cup (80ml) cold water

salt and freshly ground black pepper

2 cups (350g) cooked chickpeas

1 tsp curry powder

1 tsp garam masala

1 tbsp vegetable oil

10 popadams, cooked according to instructions

2 cups (225g) shredded mozzarella cheese

½ cup (125g) mango chutney

¼ cup (30g) diced red onion

1 large lime, cut into 6 wedges

## Make it vegan

Use a soy mozzarella-style cheese alternative or nut cheese (see page 37) instead of mozzarella.

## Make it with meat

Add 4½oz (125g) cooked chopped chicken with the chickpeas in step 3.

# Chickpea Flour Socca with Herb and Green Olive Salad

Socca—a chickpea flour pancake—hails from the south of France. Its mild, nutty flavor is the perfect canvas for the fresh herbs and flavors of the arugula salad.

**serves** 2   **prep** 5 min, plus 1 hr for batter to rest   **cook** 15 min

1   To make the batter, in a medium mixing bowl add the chickpea flour, paprika, garlic powder, salt, 2 tablespoons oil, and water. Whisk to combine. Let rest at room temperature for 1 hour.

2   With the rack in the middle of the oven, place two 8in (20cm) cast-iron or ovenproof frying pans in the oven and preheat to 450°F (230°C). (The pans will heat up with the oven.)

3   When the frying pans are heated, carefully remove and swirl 1½ teaspoons oil around in each. Pour half the batter into each and return to the oven. Bake for 8 minutes. Then turn the grill onto a low setting and cook for an additional 2 minutes. Remove and let rest for 1–2 minutes.

4   Meanwhile, to make the herb and olive salad, toss together the arugula, parsley, basil, olives, and lemon juice. Place each socca on a serving plate and top with an equal amount of salad. Serve immediately.

1 cup (100g) chickpea flour

1 tsp smoked paprika

⅛ tsp garlic powder

pinch of salt

3 tbsp olive oil

1 cup (240ml) water

2 cups (45g) arugula

½ cup (10g) flat-leaf parsley

¼ cup (5g) basil

10 (45g) pitted green olives, halved

juice of 1 lemon

## Make it with meat

To turn this into a meal, top the salad with sliced, grilled steak.

# Savory Green Pancakes with Feta and Sprout Salad

This recipe is inspired by okonomiyaki, a Japanese street food. Prepare the sprout salad with the herbs of your choice.

**makes** 4   **prep** 10 min   **cook** 15 min

1  In a large bowl, whisk together the flour and baking powder with a pinch of salt and pepper. Add the egg and then the vegetable stock, a little at a time, whisking constantly to produce a smooth, thick batter. Add the cabbage, mung beans, spring onions, and dill, and mix until completely combined.

2  In a nonstick frying pan, heat a bit of butter and olive oil over medium heat until the butter sizzles. Scoop one-quarter of the batter into the pan and use a spatula to press it into a firm, even pancake. Cook over medium-low heat for 3–4 minutes.

3  When the underside is brown and crispy, slide the pancake onto a plate. Add more butter and oil to the pan and carefully flip the pancake back into the pan to cook the other side for 3–4 minutes. Remove from the pan and keep the pancake warm while you cook 3 more, using the same process.

4  Toss the sprouts with the herbs, dress with the lemon juice and the 1 tbsp of olive oil, and season with salt and pepper. Gently crumble in the feta cheese. Serve the pancakes immediately, topped with the sprout salad.

⅓ cup (60g) all-purpose flour

¼ tsp baking powder

salt and freshly ground black pepper

1 large egg, lightly beaten

⅓ cup (85ml) vegetable stock

2 heaped cups (100g) de-ribbed and shredded savoy cabbage

1 cup (100g) sprouted mung beans

4 spring onions, finely sliced

2 tbsp finely chopped dill

unsalted butter, for frying

1 tbsp olive oil, plus extra for frying

2 cups (60g) mixed mustard, red clover, and alfalfa sprouts

handful of mixed herbs, chopped

½ tbsp lemon juice

½ cup (100g) crumbled feta cheese

## Make it vegan

Mix together 1 tbsp flax seeds with 3 tbsp warm water, let it sit for 15 minutes, and use this instead of the egg in step 1. Simply omit the feta or use a nut cheese (see page 37) instead.

# Burgers, Tacos, and Wraps

Reducing your meat intake doesn't mean you have to stop eating burgers! Enjoy a variety of vegetarian burger recipes, as well as new ways to make tacos, quesadillas, and wraps.

# Mung Bean Burgers with Red Curry Aioli

Mung beans provide this textured veggie burger with great bite and a lovely green color.

**serves** 6　**prep** 25 min　**cook** 25 min

1　Preheat the oven to 375°F (190°C). Line a baking sheet with parchment paper or spray with cooking spray. In a large mixing bowl, combine the shallot, garlic, mung beans, ground coriander, red pepper flakes, cilantro, and mint. With a pastry cutter or the back of a fork, lightly mash the mixture, allowing about half the mung beans to remain intact.

2　Add the eggs and stir to mix thoroughly. Gently fold in the breadcrumbs and season with salt and pepper.

3　Divide the mung bean mixture into 6 equal portions. Use a measuring cup to place a rounded portion onto the baking sheet and lightly flatten it to make a burger. Repeat to make 6 in total. Bake for 10 minutes on each side, carefully turning in between.

4　Meanwhile, to make the aioli, in a small mixing bowl whisk together the yogurt and red curry paste. Season with salt and pepper to taste.

5　To assemble, spread the curry aioli on the bottom half of the bun or inside the pita and add the burger. Repeat for the remaining burgers and serve immediately.

1 shallot, finely chopped

1 clove garlic, finely chopped

2 cups (350g) cooked mung beans

¼ tsp ground coriander

pinch red pepper flakes

2 tbsp chopped cilantro

1 tbsp chopped mint

2 large eggs, beaten

⅓ cup (20g) panko breadcrumbs

salt and freshly ground black pepper

½ cup (100g) plain Greek yogurt

½ tbsp red curry paste

6 hamburger buns or small pitas

## Why not try ...

For a double dose of legumes and texture, top your burger with alfalfa sprouts.

### Make it vegan

Mix 2 tbsp flax seeds with 6 tbsp warm water and let it sit for 15 minutes to replace the eggs in step 2. Replace the Greek yogurt with coconut yogurt (see page 38).

# Black-Eyed Pea Sliders with Pico de Gallo

The pico de gallo adds a wonderful texture and moisture to these creamy black-eyed pea burgers.

**serves** 8   **prep** 30 min   **cook** 20 min

1  Preheat the oven to 300°F (150°C). In a large nonstick frying pan, heat the oil over medium-low heat until shimmering. Add half the onions and cook for 2 minutes, or until soft. Add the garlic and half the jalapeño. Cook for 2 minutes. Transfer to a large mixing bowl and set aside. Set aside the frying pan, leaving any residual oil in the pan.

2  Add the chipotle chili powder, cumin, black-eyed peas, eggs, and breadcrumbs to the vegetable mixture. With a potato masher, mix to combine and break up the peas slightly.

3  Return the frying pan to the stove and heat over medium heat. Divide the mixture into 8 equal portions and use your hands to form into patties. In batches, cook for 3–4 minutes on each side, pressing lightly with a spatula to sear. Transfer the patties to a baking sheet. Repeat to use all the mixture, adding ½ teaspoon oil to the frying pan between batches. Transfer the baking sheet to the oven and bake for 8–10 minutes until cooked through.

4  Meanwhile, to make the pico de gallo, in a small bowl combine the tomato, the remaining onion, remaining jalapeño, cilantro, and lime juice. To assemble, place each burger on a slider bun and top with 1 tablespoon of pico de gallo. Serve immediately.

1 tbsp plus 1 tsp olive oil

2 small onions, diced

1 clove garlic, finely chopped

2 small jalapeños, seeded and diced, about 3 tbsp in total

½ tsp chipotle chili powder

2½ tsp ground cumin

2½ cups (450g) cooked black-eyed peas

2 large eggs, beaten

⅓ cup (20g) panko breadcrumbs

1 large tomato, seeded and diced

¼ cup (10g) chopped cilantro

juice of 1 large lime

8 slider-sized burger buns

**Why not try ...**

Give these sliders more crunch by topping with shredded green or red cabbage.

### Make it with meat

To add smokiness, finely dice 1 bacon slice and cook along with the garlic and jalapeño in step 1.

# Bean Burgers with Raw Cashew Mayo

These filling burgers can be made with any type of firm legume, such as lentils, navy beans, or chickpeas.

**serves** 4   **prep** 15 min, plus chilling   **cook** 1 hr

1   Place the beans in a saucepan of cold water and bring to a boil. Reduce heat to a simmer and cook for 35–40 minutes until soft. Drain and rinse the beans; set aside to cool.

2   In a nonstick frying pan, heat 2 tablespoons of the canola oil over medium heat. Add the mushrooms and cook for 5–7 minutes, until they are cooked through. Set aside to cool.

3   Put the beans, mushrooms, breadcrumbs, onion, parsley, Worcestershire sauce, and egg into a food processor and season with salt and pepper. Pulse the mixture until it is just mixed but still has some texture. With damp hands, shape the mixture into 4 patties and chill, covered, for 1 hour.

4   To make the cashew mayo, drain the cashews and place them in a food processor with the lemon juice, olive oil, garlic, and 5–6 tbsp of water. Process until smooth, then chill until needed.

5   In a large nonstick frying pan, heat the remaining 2 tbsp canola oil over medium heat. Cook the burger patties for 3–4 minutes on each side, until well browned and cooked through. Serve immediately on toasted buns, topped with avocado and tomato slices, alfalfa sprouts, and the cashew mayo.

3 cups (450g) mixed beans

4 tbsp canola oil

1 cup (60g) finely diced cremini mushrooms

1½ cups (150g) fresh white breadcrumbs

½ small onion, finely grated

2 tbsp finely chopped flat-leaf parsley

2 tsp Worcestershire sauce

1 large egg, lightly beaten

salt and freshly ground black pepper

1 cup (120g) raw cashews, soaked for 3 hours

2 tbsp lemon juice

1 tbsp olive oil

1 small clove garlic, crushed

**To serve**

4 hamburger buns, toasted

sliced avocado and tomato

handful of alfalfa sprouts

## Make it vegan

Mix 1 tbsp of flax seeds with 3 tbsp water and let it sit for 15 minutes to replace the egg in step 3.

# Seeded Beet and Buckwheat Burgers

These hearty and earthy vegetarian burgers combine the sweetness of beets and the nutty texture of seeds with wholesome buckwheat. You won't miss the meat with these!

**serves** 4   **prep** 15 min, plus soaking and chilling   **cook** 30 min

1  Place the buckwheat in a large bowl and cover with water. Cover the bowl with a kitchen towel and leave to soak for at least 8 hours or for up to 12 hours. Then drain and rinse under running water.

2  Place the beets, carrots, and onions in a food processor and pulse for 1–2 minutes to combine. Then add the buckwheat, eggs, oats, and salt and pulse until just incorporated.

3  Add all but 1 tablespoon of the sunflower seeds to the mixture, pulse to combine, and transfer to a large bowl. Add the remaining sunflower seeds and stir to combine. Chill in the fridge for 30 minutes. Divide the mixture into 4 equal portions, then shape each portion into a 4in (9cm) wide and ¾in (2cm) thick burger patty.

4  Heat the oil in a nonstick frying pan over medium-high heat. Once the oil is hot, add the patties and fry for about 5 minutes on each side or until firm and lightly colored. Do this in batches to avoid overcrowding the pan. Remove from the heat and drain on a plate lined with paper towel. Serve with burger buns, mayonnaise, chips, and a green salad.

⅓ cup (60g) uncooked buckwheat

1 cup (125g) unpeeled and coarsely chopped beets

⅔ cup (85g) unpeeled and coarsely chopped carrots

⅓ cup (30g) trimmed and finely chopped spring onions

2 eggs

⅓ cup (60g) oats

½ tsp salt

½ cup (60g) sunflower seeds

2–3 tbsp vegetable oil

**Why not try ...**

Use pumpkin seeds in place of the sunflower seeds.

**Make it vegan**

Mix 2 tbsp flax seeds with 6 tbsp warm water and let it sit for 15 minutes to replace the eggs in step 2.

# Veggie Burger with Spelt

These vegetarian burgers get their intense flavor from the super-absorbent spelt grain. Roasting the vegetables before they are added to the burgers helps retain more of their flavor and keeps the unnecessary moisture out.

**serves** 6  **prep** 15 min, plus overnight soaking and chilling  **cook** 1 hr

1  Place the spelt in a bowl, cover with water, and leave to soak overnight. Then drain well and rinse under running water. Place the spelt in a lidded saucepan. Pour in 1 cup (240ml) of water and bring to a boil. Then reduce the heat to a simmer, cover, and cook for 50 minutes. Remove from the heat and set aside to cool.

2  Preheat the oven to 425°F (220°C). Spread out the mushrooms on a lined baking sheet and toss with 2 teaspoons of the tamari. Spread out the beets, carrots, and beans on a separate sheet. Season with salt and pepper and toss with the oil. Place the sheets in the oven and bake for about 15 minutes. Then remove from the heat and lightly toss the vegetables and mushrooms. Return to the oven, rotating the positions of the sheets. Bake for a further 10 minutes or until the vegetables and beans are crisp and the mushrooms have lost most of their moisture. Remove from the heat and leave to cool.

3  Place the ground almonds, breadcrumbs, cooled vegetables, and remaining tamari in a food processor and pulse until just combined. Add the mustard, mayonnaise, spring onions, garlic, and eggs to the mixture. Season to taste with pepper and pulse to combine. Then add the spelt and tempeh and pulse lightly until just mixed, but still retaining some texture. Transfer the mixture to a large bowl, cover, and chill in the fridge for about 1 hour.

4  Set the grill or griddle pan to medium-low. Divide the mixture into 6 equal portions and form each into a 1in- (2.5cm-) thick patty. Grill the patties for about 5 minutes on each side, until crisp on the outside. Remove from the heat. Serve hot in burger buns, topped with avocado, tomato, and onion slices.

¼ cup (40g) uncooked spelt grains (available from health food stores)

1½ cups (140g) sliced shiitake mushrooms

3 tsp tamari or low-sodium soy sauce

1 large beet, about 1 cup (100g), grated

2 large carrots, about 1 cup (100g), grated

14oz (400g) can kidney beans, drained

salt and freshly ground black pepper

1–2 tbsp olive oil

½ cup (50g) ground almonds

⅓ cup (40g) panko breadcrumbs

2 tbsp spicy Dijon mustard

2 tbsp mayonnaise

2 spring onions, sliced

2 cloves garlic, pressed

2 large eggs

4oz (115g) tempeh, crumbled

**For serving**

6 burger buns

1 avocado, pitted, peeled, and sliced

1 large tomato, sliced into rounds

1 large red onion, sliced into rounds

### Make it vegan

Mix 2 tbsp flax seeds with 6 tbsp warm water and let it sit for 15 minutes to replace the eggs in step 3. Substitute a vegan mayonnaise (see page 39), too.

# Pinto Bean and Spiralized Sweet Potato Quesadilla

This quesadilla is a great combination of heat from the jalapeño and sweetness from the potato. Spiralizing the sweet potato adds texture to this Mexican snack.

**makes** 4   **prep** 20 min   **cook** 40 min

1  With the medium blade of a spiralizer, spiralize the sweet potato.

2  In a medium frying pan, heat the oil over medium-low heat until shimmering. Add the jalapeño and cook for 3 minutes, or until tender but not brown. Add the sweet potato and cook for 7 minutes, or until just al dente.

3  To assemble, place 1 tortilla on a clean, flat surface. Sprinkle about ¼ cup (30g) Cheddar on the lower half of the tortilla. Top with a quarter of the pinto beans and a quarter of the sweet potato. Add 2 tablespoons of onion and 2 tablespoons of cilantro. Top with about another ¼ cup (30g) Cheddar, then fold over the top of the tortilla to create a semicircle. Repeat to make 4 quesadillas in total.

4  Heat a nonstick frying pan over medium heat. Add 1 quesadilla and cook for 4 minutes. Carefully turn, cover, and cook for another 4 minutes, until the tortilla is golden and the cheese melted. Repeat for the remaining 3 quesadillas.

5  Cut each quesadilla into 4 sections. Serve immediately with sour cream on the side.

1 small sweet potato, peeled

2 tbsp vegetable oil

1 jalapeño, seeded and diced

4 large flour tortillas

2 cups (225g) finely shredded sharp Cheddar cheese

1⅓ cups (200g) cooked pinto or borlotti beans

½ cup (45g) chopped spring onion

½ cup (15g) chopped cilantro

sour cream, to serve

## Make it with meat

Layer 1oz (30g) cooked, chopped chicken or pork on top of the sweet potato in step 3.

# Greek White Bean Tacos

This twist on the traditional taco features ingredients typically found in a Greek salad. Romaine lettuce and cucumber add freshness and crunch to the creamy white beans and feta.

**makes** 8  **prep** 25 min  **cook** 1 hr

1  In a small casserole or saucepan, heat the oil over medium-low heat. Add the garlic and cook for 1–2 minutes until soft but not brown. Add the navy beans, lemon zest and juice, and stock.

2  Bring to a simmer then reduce the heat to low and cook, covered, for 5–6 minutes, until the stock has been absorbed. Stir in the oregano. Season with salt and pepper to taste.

3  To assemble, spread 1 tablespoon of yogurt on a tortilla. Divide the bean mixture into 8 portions and add one portion to the tortilla. Top with a portion of lettuce, then tomato, and cucumber. Sprinkle the feta on top. Repeat with the remaining 7 tortillas, fold, and serve immediately.

2 tbsp olive oil

1 clove garlic, crushed

2 cups (450g) cooked navy beans

zest and juice of 1 large lemon

¼ cup (60ml) vegetable stock

1 tbsp chopped oregano

salt and freshly ground black pepper

½ cup (100g) plain Greek yogurt

8 small corn or flour tortillas

2½ cups (85g) shredded romaine lettuce

2 cups (350g) diced Roma tomatoes

1 cup (140g) diced English cucumber

4oz (115g) crumbled feta cheese

### Make it with meat

Add 2½oz (75g) cooked, chopped shrimp or chicken along with the beans in step 1.

# Quinoa Falafel with Mint Yogurt Sauce

The addition of quinoa to the traditional falafel gives them an added whole grain goodness and a unique flavor and texture. It is paired here with a fresh and light yogurt sauce to complement the earthy spices.

**serves** 4  **prep** 15 min, plus chilling  **cook** 45 min

1 Rinse the quinoa under running water, place in a large saucepan, and cover with ⅔ cup (170ml) of water. Place the pan over medium heat and bring to a simmer. Cook the quinoa for 15 minutes or until almost all the water has been absorbed. Remove from the heat, drain any remaining water, and set aside.

2 Place the quinoa, egg, garlic, cumin, salt, and ½ cup (350g) of the chickpeas in a food processor. Pulse until well combined. Add the cilantro and the remaining chickpeas and pulse lightly for 1 minute, until the chickpeas have broken down but still retain some of their texture. Transfer the mixture to a large bowl and chill in the fridge for 30 minutes.

3 Preheat the oven to 400°F (200°C). Grease and line a baking sheet with parchment paper. Divide the falafel mixture into eight equal portions. On a lightly floured surface, roll each portion into a smooth ball and press down lightly to form patty-like shapes.

4 Brush the falafel with a little oil on both sides and place on the baking sheet. Bake in the oven for 20 minutes or until the falafel are well browned and crispy on the outside. Remove from the heat.

5 For the sauce, place all the ingredients in a bowl and mix well. Serve the falafel and mint yogurt sauce with pita breads and a green salad.

⅓ cup (60g) uncooked quinoa

1 egg

2 cloves garlic

1 tbsp cumin

¼ tsp salt

2 (14oz/400g) cans chickpeas, drained

4 tbsp chopped cilantro

1 tbsp all-purpose flour, for dusting

1–2 tbsp olive oil, plus extra for greasing

**For the sauce**

⅔ cup (150g) Greek yogurt

4 tbsp chopped mint

juice of 1 lemon

### Make it vegan

Reserve 3 tbsp liquid before you drain the chickpeas. Add this instead of the egg in step 2. Substitute coconut yogurt (see page 38) for the sauce.

# Baked Falafel with Pickled Red Onions

For a healthier version of the Middle Eastern street snack, this falafel is oven-baked instead of fried. Pickled onions and sambal oelek are the perfect tangy-sweet and spicy condiments.

**serves** 16  **prep** 30 min, plus 3 hr to chill  **cook** 40 min

1  To make the pickled red onions, in a medium saucepan bring the apple cider vinegar, red wine vinegar, sugar, and salt to a boil over medium heat. Stir until the sugar and salt dissolve. Remove from the heat and stir in the red onion. Leave to cool completely at room temperature, stirring occasionally. Pour into a glass jar and secure with a lid. Refrigerate for 3 hours or overnight.

2  Preheat the oven to 400°F (200°C). In a food processor, combine the garlic, chickpeas, baking soda, coriander, cumin, red pepper flakes, parsley, cilantro, and lemon zest and juice. Pulse until combined but not smooth.

3  Transfer the chickpea mixture to a medium mixing bowl and fold in the chickpea flour. Drizzle oil over and stir until it holds together. Season with salt and pepper to taste.

4  Portion out approximately 2 tablespoons of chickpea mixture and roll into a ball with your hands. Place on a baking sheet and repeat with the remaining mixture. With a spatula, slightly flatten each one. Bake for 10 minutes, turn over, and bake for an additional 10 minutes. Serve immediately with the pickled red onions and sambal oelek on the side.

1 cup (240ml) apple cider vinegar

½ cup (120ml) red wine vinegar

2 tbsp sugar

1 tsp salt

1 large red onion, thinly sliced

1 clove garlic

2 cups (350g) cooked chickpeas

½ tsp baking soda

½ tsp ground coriander

½ tsp ground cumin

pinch red pepper flakes

1 bunch curly parsley, chopped

1¼ cups (20g) finely chopped cilantro

zest and juice of 1 lemon

¼ cup (20g) chickpea flour

1 tbsp olive oil

salt and freshly ground black pepper

⅓ cup (75g) sambal oelek

## Why not try ...

If you'd rather skip the heat, serve with tzatziki sauce instead of spicy sambal.

### Make it with meat

Add 8oz (225g) raw minced lamb along with the olive oil in step 3.

# Salads

Perfect to enjoy as a filling lunch or as a delicious
side to your main meal, these fresh, bright salads
will make it easy to eat your five servings a day.

# Thai Noodle Salad

Making your own quick pickles is easy, and their refreshing, sharp flavors can really finish a dish. Lotus root is beautiful, but normal radishes work just as well.

**serves** 6  **prep** 30 min, plus pickling  **cook** none

**1** To make the pickled lotus: soak the lotus root in cold water for 20 to 30 minutes. Drain, then blanch in boiling water for 1 to 2 minutes. Drain and refresh under cold water, then stack the slices in a small glass jar. Whisk together the rice wine vinegar, sugar, and salt until the sugar has dissolved. Pour the vinegar mixture over the lotus root, cover, and refrigerate for at least 1 day and up to 5 days before using.

**2** To make the dressing: whisk together all the ingredients, along with 2 tablespoons water, until the sugar has dissolved.

**3** Place the noodles in a heatproof bowl and cover with boiling water. Soak for 15 minutes until soft, and snip with kitchen scissors to make a more manageable length to eat. Drain, rinse well under cold water, and set aside to cool and drain completely.

**4** In a large bowl, combine the cooled noodles with the finely sliced vegetables, dried shrimp, and most of the chopped herbs and peanuts. Add the dressing and toss very well until the dressing is completely incorporated.

**5** Heap the salad into the middle of a serving bowl and scatter with the reserved herbs and peanuts. Top with the pickled lotus root and serve immediately with any extra dressing and lotus root on the side.

8oz (225g) dried glass noodles

1½ cups (225g) julienned green papaya or green mango

2 carrots, julienned

½ small red onion, very finely sliced

2 under-ripe tomatoes, halved and cut into very thin wedges

2 tbsp dried shrimp, very finely chopped or crushed with a mortar and pestle

handful mint, coarsely chopped

handful cilantro, coarsely chopped

2 tbsp salted peanuts, coarsely chopped

**For the pickled lotus**

1 lotus root, peeled and thinly sliced, about 3½oz (100g) in total

½ cup (120ml) rice wine vinegar

¼ cup (50g) sugar

1 tsp fine sea salt

**For the dressing**

4 tsp sugar

4 tbsp lime juice

2 tbsp fish sauce

2 tbsp rice wine vinegar

1 clove garlic, crushed

### Make it vegan

Simply omit the dried shrimp, and use a vegan fish sauce or soy sauce in the dressing in place of fish sauce.

### Make it with meat

Add 6oz (180g) cooked, chopped chicken with the noodles, dried shrimp, herbs, and peanuts in step 4.

# Rainbow Bowl with Sesame and Ginger Dressing

To maximize the visual impact of the colorful, fresh ingredients, serve this salad with the vegetables displayed in sections and the dressing in a bowl alongside ready to toss at the table.

**serves** 4   **prep** 10 min   **cook** none

1   To make the dressing: whisk all the ingredients together. For a more emulsified finish, blend them in a small blender or food processor.

2   Spiralize the carrots, beet, cucumber, and squash. Divide the spiralized vegetables evenly among 4 bowls, laying out the vegetables in contrasting piles. Scatter each serving with the sesame seeds and cilantro. Serve with the dressing and lime halves alongside.

2 thick carrots, trimmed and peeled

1 medium beet, peeled

½ English cucumber, trimmed

2 small summer squash or yellow heritage carrots, trimmed

1 tsp black sesame seeds, to garnish

cilantro, to garnish

lime halves, to serve

### For the dressing

2 tbsp sunflower oil

2 tbsp lime juice

2 tsp sesame oil

2 tsp soy sauce

2 tsp honey

1 clove garlic, crushed

1in (2.5cm) piece fresh ginger, peeled and finely grated

½ small shallot, finely chopped

## Make it vegan

Replace the honey in the dressing with agave nectar or rice malt syrup.

# Spicy Tahini Black Rice Noodle Salad

This stunning salad is tasty on its own as a light lunch or side dish, or topped with grilled teriyaki-glazed salmon as a main dish. Caramelized pumpkin seeds add a sweet and spicy crunch.

**serves** 4-6   **prep** 30 min   **cook** 5 min

1. Preheat the oven to 350°F (180°C) and line a baking sheet with parchment paper. To make the caramelized pumpkin seeds: in a small bowl, whisk together the sunflower oil, brown sugar, salt, and chili powder. Add the pumpkin seeds and toss to coat thoroughly, then spread on the prepared baking sheet. Bake on the top rack of the oven for around 5 minutes, until the seeds begin to brown and stick together. Remove from the oven and spread on a plate to cool. Once cool, break up any clumps.

2. To make the dressing: whisk together all the ingredients along with 2 tablespoons cold water until completely combined. Set aside.

3. Cook the noodles according to the package instructions. Then drain, rinse well under cold water, and drain again. Toss with a drizzle of sunflower oil to prevent sticking. Allow to cool completely.

4. Use a potato peeler to peel wide ribbons of carrot into a serving bowl. Add the cabbage, spring onions, and most of the pumpkin seeds and cilantro, along with the cooled noodles. Add the dressing and toss well to combine.

5. Heap the salad in the center of the serving bowl. Sprinkle with the reserved pumpkin seeds and cilantro. Season with salt and pepper to taste, and serve immediately.

10oz (300g) dried black rice noodles

sunflower oil, to toss

2 large carrots, peeled

2¾ cups (200g) shredded red cabbage

4 spring onions, julienned

handful cilantro, finely chopped

salt and freshly ground black pepper

### For the pumpkin seeds

1 tsp sunflower oil

1 tbsp light brown sugar

pinch salt

pinch chili powder

½ cup (60g) raw shelled pumpkin seeds

### For the dressing

2 tbsp tahini

2 tbsp sunflower oil

1 tsp chili oil

2 tbsp lime juice

1 tbsp soy sauce

1 tbsp agave nectar

### Make it with fish

For a main dish, top each salad with 3½oz (100g) grilled teriyaki-glazed salmon. Make the teriyaki glaze by combining ½ cup (125ml) each of water, mirin, soy sauce, and sugar in a saucepan. Bring the mixture to a boil and stir until the sugar has dissolved. Simmer for 10–15 minutes or until the sauce thickens.

# Vietnamese Chicken Noodle Salad

Based on the traditional Vietnamese dish of "bún," this refreshing noodle salad is tossed in a zesty citrus dressing and topped with chicken flavored with ginger and lemongrass.

**serves** 4   **prep** 45 min, plus marinating   **cook** 15 min

1  To make the marinade: place all the ingredients in the bowl of a food processor and process until smooth.

2  With a rolling pin or meat mallet, pound the chicken thighs to flatten them to even thicknesses. Place in a shallow dish and add the marinade. Using your hands, rub the marinade into the chicken. Refrigerate, covered, for at least 2 hours and up to 12 hours.

3  To make the dressing: whisk together all the ingredients until the sugar has dissolved. Then whisk in 4 tablespoons cold water and set aside.

4  Place the noodles in a large, heatproof bowl and cover with boiling water. Leave to soak for 15 minutes until soft. Drain, rinse well under cold water, and drain again. Set aside to cool and drain completely.

5  Preheat the broiler on high. Line a large, rimmed baking sheet with foil and arrange the marinated chicken in a single layer. Broil the chicken for 5 to 7 minutes on each side until dark brown and crispy in places. Set aside to cool slightly.

6  Divide the lettuce evenly among 4 bowls and top each bowl with an equal amount of noodles, spiralized cucumber and carrot, and bean sprouts. Lightly toss the ingredients in each bowl.

7  Top each bowl with 1 chicken thigh, sliced on the diagonal. Sprinkle with spring onions, mint, Thai basil, and peanuts. Serve immediately with the dressing on the side.

### Make it vegan

Replace the chicken with 1lb (450g) firm tofu cut into four pieces. Marinate the tofu according to step 2. Sear the pieces in a nonstick pan until they're golden brown and caramelized around the edges. Use extra soy sauce instead of fish sauce, too.

4 large boneless, skinless chicken thighs

10oz (300g) dried rice vermicelli

1 heart romaine lettuce, trimmed and shredded

¼ English cucumber, spiralized

1 large, thick carrot, spiralized

2 large handfuls bean sprouts

4 spring onions, finely sliced

handful mint, lightly chopped

handful Thai basil, lightly chopped

2 heaped tbsp salted peanuts, coarsely chopped

**For the marinade**

1 large or 2 small stalks lemongrass, peeled, trimmed, and finely chopped

½in (1.5cm) piece fresh ginger, peeled and coarsely chopped

1 clove garlic, coarsely chopped

1 tbsp coarsely chopped cilantro stems

2 tbsp sunflower oil

1 tbsp lime juice

2 tsp light brown sugar

2 tsp soy sauce

2 tsp fish sauce

**For the dressing**

4 tbsp lemon juice

4 tsp fish sauce

3 tsp sugar

1 clove garlic, crushed

pinch white pepper

# Mung Bean Gado Gado

Gado Gado is an Indonesian chopped salad whose name means "mix mix." It's always served with spicy peanut dressing, and is accompanied here by crisp vegetables and pulses.

**serves** 4   **prep** 45 min   **cook** none

1  To make the spicy peanut dressing, in a small bowl whisk together the peanut butter, garlic powder, ginger, red pepper flakes, soy sauce, lime juice, and vinegar. Stir in the water until thoroughly mixed. Set aside.

2  Adjust a spiralizer to the thinnest blade and spiralize the beet.

3  On a large serving plate, spread the cabbage in an even layer. On top of the cabbage, arrange in separate piles the cooked mung beans, cherry tomatoes, sprouted mung beans, spiralized beet, green beans, and hard-boiled eggs. Serve immediately with the dressing on the side.

½ cup (125g) creamy peanut butter

1 tsp garlic powder

1½ tsp ground ginger

1 tsp red pepper flakes

1½ tsp soy sauce

juice of 2 limes

1 tsp rice wine vinegar

¾ cup (180ml) water

1 small beet, peeled

2 cups (150g) shredded Savoy cabbage

½ cup (85g) cooked mung beans

½ cup (85g) halved cherry tomatoes

½ cup (30g) sprouted mung beans (bean sprouts)

½ cup (75g) chopped green beans, blanched and drained

2 hard-boiled eggs, quartered

## Why not try ...

Use an equal amount of chickpeas in place of the cooked mung beans.

### Make it vegan

Replace the eggs with 1 cup (225g) cubed and seared tempeh or tofu.

### Make it with meat

Add to the serving plate 6oz (170g) thinly sliced, pan-seared steak.

# Roasted Carrots and Chickpeas

Vadouvan, or French masala, is a curry spice blend originating from Southern India. Cool yogurt tempers the spice and pairs well with the sweetness of roasted carrots.

**serves** 4   **prep** 15 min   **cook** 30 min

**1** Preheat the oven to 350°F (150°C). Arrange the carrots in a single layer on a baking tray and drizzle with olive oil. Roast for 25–30 minutes until tender.

**2** Meanwhile, in a small mixing bowl, toss together the chickpeas, vinegar, garlic, thyme, and red pepper flakes. Season with salt and pepper. Set aside.

**3** In another small mixing bowl, stir together the Greek yogurt and vadouvan.

**4** Spread the yogurt on a serving plate, arrange the roasted carrots over the yogurt, and top with the chickpea mixture. Garnish with ground pepper and the reserved carrot leaves. Serve immediately.

1 lb (450g) whole young carrots, leafy tops chopped and reserved for garnish

2 tbsp olive oil

2 cups (350g) cooked chickpeas

2 tsp red wine vinegar

1 clove garlic, finely chopped

1 tsp thyme leaves

pinch red pepper flakes

salt and freshly ground black pepper

¾ cup (150g) plain Greek yogurt

1 tbsp vadouvan (French masala)

## Why not try ...

If you can't find vadouvan, replace it with curry powder which contains many of the same ingredients found in vadouvan.

### Make it vegan

Substitute an equal amount of coconut yogurt (see page 38) for the Greek yogurt.

# Avocado, Cilantro, and Lime Tabbouleh

Tabbouleh is traditionally served as part of a mezze in the Middle East, but it also makes an excellent salad on its own or to accompany cold meats. The lime and avocado in this version give it a fresh dimension.

**serves** 4  **prep** 15 min, plus soaking and chilling  **cook** none

1  Place 1½ cups (350ml) of water in a large saucepan and bring to a boil. Place the bulgur wheat and rock salt in a large bowl. Pour over the boiling water, cover, and leave to soak for about 30 minutes.

2  Drain any excess water from the bulgur wheat and place it in a large bowl. Then add the tomatoes, avocado, red pepper, onion, and cilantro. Mix well to combine. Transfer the mixture to a large serving bowl.

3  Drizzle the lime juice and oil over the mixture. Toss well to coat. Season to taste with salt and pepper, if needed. Mix well and chill the tabbouleh in the fridge for about 20 minutes before serving.

1¼ cups (175g) bulgur wheat

1½ tsp rock salt

2 tomatoes, diced

1 avocado, pitted, peeled, and diced

1 small red pepper, seeded and diced

⅓ cup (60g) diced red onion

handful cilantro, coarsely chopped

½ cup (125ml) lime juice

2 tbsp extra virgin olive oil

salt and freshly ground black pepper

### Make it with meat

This tabbouleh can be topped with grilled, sliced steak for a more filling meal.

# Sweet Potato and Beluga Lentil Salad

The firm nuttiness of the lentils and the soft, caramelized sweet potato makes a wonderful combination of flavors and textures.

**serves** 2  **prep** 25 min, plus cooling  **cook** 45 min

1  Preheat the oven to 350°F (180°C). On a baking sheet, toss the sweet potato and paprika in 1 tablespoon of oil. Season with salt and pepper. Roast until tender and slightly caramelized, about 25 minutes, stirring once halfway. Let cool to room temperature.

2  Meanwhile, in a medium saucepan, bring the water to a boil. Add the lentils and return to a boil for 2–3 minutes. Reduce to a simmer and cook, covered, for 25–30 minutes, until tender but not soft. Drain in a fine colander and let cool to room temperature.

3  To assemble, in a large mixing bowl combine the lentils, sweet potatoes, onion, celery, and feta. Mix well. Drizzle in the honey, lemon juice, and remaining 1 tablespoon of oil. Toss to combine. Season with salt and pepper to taste. Garnish with the reserved celery leaves. Serve at room temperature.

1 large sweet potato, peeled and cubed

⅛ tsp smoked paprika

2 tbsp olive oil

salt and freshly ground black pepper

3 cups (750ml) water

1½ cups (325g) uncooked beluga lentils

2 spring onions, trimmed and thinly sliced

1 large celery stalk, diced, leafy parts reserved for garnish

¼ cup (30g) crumbled feta cheese

1 tbsp honey or agave nectar

juice of 1 lemon

## Why not try ...

Substitute an equal amount uncooked brown or green lentils for the beluga lentils.

### Make it vegan

Use a nut-based vegan cheese alternative rather than feta.

### Make it with meat

Add 4 crumbled slices of crispy bacon to the lentil-feta mixture in step 3.

# Lima Bean Panzanella

Panzanella is a Tuscan bread salad popular in the warmer months. It's a great use for day-old bread and wonderful for parties and picnics, as it can be served at room temperature.

**serves** 6   **prep** 25 min   **cook** 15 min

1  Preheat the oven to 325°F (170°C). Cut the bread into ½in (1cm) cubes. On a baking sheet, arrange the bread cubes in a single layer and bake for 15 minutes, or until toasted and light golden brown.

2  Meanwhile, to make the dressing, in a small bowl whisk together the vinegar and Dijon mustard. While whisking, drizzle in the oil and thoroughly combine. Stir in the garlic, oregano, and basil. Set aside.

3  To assemble, in a large salad bowl, add the tomatoes, lima beans, cucumber, and corn. Fold in the toasted bread, then drizzle the dressing over. Toss to coat. Season with salt and pepper to taste. Serve immediately.

1 small loaf sourdough bread

¼ cup (60ml) red wine vinegar

1 tbsp Dijon mustard

½ cup (120ml) olive oil

2 cloves garlic, finely chopped

1 tsp chopped oregano

1 tsp chopped basil

1⅛ cups (175g) halved cherry tomatoes

1¼ cups (225g) cooked lima beans

1 English cucumber, diced

1 cup (150g) fresh corn kernels

salt and freshly ground black pepper

## Make it with fish

Add 4oz (115g) cooked shrimp when you assemble the salad.

# Caprese Farro Salad

Featuring fresh summer tomatoes, soft mozzarella, chewy farro, and a homemade pesto sauce, this colorful and light Italian salad makes the perfect appetizer for any meal.

**serves** 4   **prep** 10 min, plus cooling   **cook** 50 min

1  Rinse the farro under cold running water and place in a large saucepan. Cover with about 2½ cups (600ml) of water and bring to a boil. Then reduce the heat to a simmer and cook, stirring occasionally, for about 40 minutes or until softened. Remove from the heat, drain, and set aside to cool.

2  For the pesto, place the basil, pine nuts, garlic, and oil in a food processor and pulse until smooth. Season to taste, if needed.

3  Place the mozzarella and tomatoes in a large bowl. Add the pesto and cooled farro and stir to mix. Chill the salad in the fridge until ready to serve, garnished with a few basil leaves.

1 cup (200g) uncooked farro

8oz (225g) mozzarella cheese, cubed

3 large tomatoes, cut into bite-sized pieces

**For the pesto**

1 cup (45g) basil, rinsed and dried, plus extra to garnish

2 tbsp pine nuts

1 clove garlic

2–3 tbsp extra virgin olive oil

salt

## Why not try ...

You could replace the fresh mozzarella cheese with the same quantity of burrata cheese.

### Make it vegan

Use a nut cheese (see page 37) instead of the mozzarella.

# Nutty Barley and Lentil Salad

This is no boring salad! The combination of hearty barley and nutty, crunchy almonds and walnuts is well balanced by the contrasting tastes and textures of sweet, dried cranberries and salty goat cheese.

**serves** 4   **prep** 10 min, plus overnight soaking and cooling   **cook** 30 min

1  Place the barley in a bowl, cover with water, and leave to soak overnight or for at least 8 hours. Then drain, rinse under running water, and drain well again.

2  Place the barley in a lidded saucepan and cover with plenty of water. Bring to a boil, then reduce the heat to a simmer, and cover. Cook for about 30 minutes or until the barley is tender. Remove from the heat, drain any remaining water, and leave to cool completely.

3  Once cooled, place the barley and lentils in a large bowl and mix lightly to combine. Add the almonds, walnuts, and cranberries and mix to combine. Sprinkle over the goat cheese, add the arugula, and toss lightly. Divide the salad equally between four plates and serve immediately.

⅓ cup (75g) uncooked pearl barley

14oz (400g) can green lentils, drained

¼ cup (25g) coarsely chopped almonds

¼ cup (25g) coarsely chopped walnuts

⅓ cup (50g) dried cranberries

⅓ cup (100g) crumbled soft goat cheese

5 cups (100g) arugula

## Why not try ...

You could try the same amount of sunflower seeds or chopped Brazil nuts instead of the almonds or walnuts. You could also replace the arugula with the same quantity of flat-leaf parsley.

### Make it vegan

Simply replace the soft goat cheese with nut cheese (see page 37).

# Freekeh Sweet and Spicy Warm Salad

This warming and colorful salad combines sweet roasted squash and sticky dates with a fragrant and spiced freekeh and is perfect for fall and winter lunches.

**serves** 4   **prep** 15 min, plus cooling   **cook** 40 min

1 Preheat the oven to 400°F (200°C). Place the cinnamon, ginger, cumin, and oil in a small bowl and mix to combine. Place the butternut squash on a baking sheet, pour the mixture over, and toss to coat. Bake in the oven for 30–35 minutes or until the squash is tender.

2 Meanwhile, rinse the freekeh under running water and place in a large saucepan. Cover with 4 cups (1 liter) of water and bring to a boil. Then reduce the heat to a simmer and cook for 15 minutes or until almost all the water has been absorbed. Remove from the heat, drain any remaining water, and leave to cool slightly.

3 For the dressing, place all the ingredients in a bowl. Season to taste and mix to combine. Place the radicchio and dates in a large serving dish. Add the squash and freekeh and toss lightly to mix. Then pour over the dressing, season to taste, and toss until well combined. Serve warm garnished with parsley.

2 tsp ground cinnamon

1 tsp grated ginger

1 tsp ground cumin

2 tbsp light olive oil

1 butternut squash, seeded and cut into ¾in (2cm) cubes

1 cup (200g) cracked freekeh

1 small head radicchio, coarsely chopped

8 dried pitted dates, about 1½oz (40g) in total, coarsely chopped

4 tbsp coarsely chopped flat-leaf parsley

**For the dressing**

4 tbsp extra virgin olive oil

juice of 1 lemon

1 tbsp honey

salt and freshly ground black pepper

## Why not try ...

Try using 2 large sweet potatoes in place of the squash, and cook in the same way. You can also use chicory or arugula instead of the radicchio.

### Make it vegan

Use maple syrup or agave nectar instead of honey.

# Soups and Stews

From ramen and minestrone to chili, the variety of soups and stews in this chapter are perfect for expanding your cooking repertoire and impressing dinner guests. Get into the habit of making double batches to store in the freezer, ensuring you'll always have delicious, nutritious meals on hand.

# Mushroom Miso Ramen

A light, miso-based soup, this ramen will appeal to mushroom lovers, as it contains three different types. The mushrooms bring an earthy flavor to the ramen, which pairs very well with both the tofu and miso.

**serves** 4   **prep** 10 min   **cook** 30 min

1   In a large pan over medium heat, bring the stock to a simmer.

2   Add the oyster mushrooms, shiitake mushrooms, and spring onions, and simmer for 20 minutes.

3   Add the vegetarian white miso paste, tofu, and baby spinach. Simmer for 5 minutes.

4   While the broth is simmering, in a large pan of boiling water over high heat, cook the ramen noodles for 4 minutes, stirring occasionally. Drain, rinse, and divide between 4 deep serving bowls.

5   Fill the bowls with the hot broth, just covering the noodles.

6   Add the enoki mushrooms and nori strips to each bowl, then serve.

6 cups (1.4 liters) Vegan Ramen Stock (see page 31)

½ cup (85g) sliced oyster mushrooms

½ cup (85g) shiitake mushrooms

8 spring onions, finely chopped (reserve some green for garnish)

4 tbsp vegetarian white miso paste

1 cup (175g) cubed firm tofu

1 cup (85g) baby spinach

24oz (680g) ramen noodles

1 cup (175g) fresh enoki mushrooms, trimmed

4 sheets nori, sliced into strips

# Tom Yum Ramen

Tom Yum hails from Thailand. With its light, creamy texture and citrusy flavor, this dish is balanced and refreshing. You can serve this ramen on a hot summer night with a crisp, cool drink.

**serves** 4   **prep** 25 min   **cook** 40 min

1  In a large pan over medium heat, bring the stock to a simmer.

2  Add the garlic, galangal, lemongrass, and lime leaves. Cover the pan, and simmer for 30 minutes. Strain the broth, discarding the solids.

3  Bring the broth back up to a simmer and add the Thai chili garlic paste, salt, sugar, white soy sauce, lime juice (to taste), oyster mushrooms, cherry tomatoes, tofu, and coconut milk. Simmer for 5 minutes.

4  While the broth is simmering, in a large pan of boiling water over a high heat, cook the ramen noodles for 4 minutes, stirring occasionally. Drain, rinse, and divide between 4 deep serving bowls.

5  Fill the bowls with the hot broth, just covering the noodles. Garnish each bowl with the spring onions and cilantro, and serve with the lime wedges.

6 cups (1.4 liters) Vegan Ramen Stock (see page 31)

4 cloves garlic, finely chopped

2in (5cm) piece galangal or ginger, sliced

2 whole stalks lemongrass, peeled and chopped in 3in (7.5cm) pieces

3 lime leaves

2 tsp Thai chili garlic paste

1 tsp sea salt

1½ tsp sugar

2 tbsp white soy sauce

juice of 1 lime

1 cup (175g) oyster mushrooms, trimmed

8 cherry tomatoes

1 cup (175g) cubed firm tofu

½ cup (120ml) coconut milk

24oz (680g) ramen noodles

¼ cup (45g) finely chopped spring onions

¼ cup (45g) coarsely chopped cilantro

1 lime, cut into 4 wedges

# Tomato Miso Ramen

This ramen is as comforting as a bowl of tomato soup, but with the added depth of salty miso and the addition of delicious, chewy noodles.

**serves** 4  **prep** 20 min  **cook** 15 min

1 In a large pan over medium heat, bring the stock to a simmer.

2 Chop the tomatoes into bite-sized pieces, and add to the broth.

3 Add the tomato paste, sugar, and white soy sauce. Simmer for 5 minutes.

4 Add the vegetarian red miso paste and chili bean paste. Simmer for 5 minutes.

5 While the broth is simmering, in a large pan of boiling water over high heat, cook the ramen noodles for 4 minutes, stirring occasionally. Drain, rinse, and divide between 4 deep serving bowls.

6 Fill the bowls with the hot broth, just covering the noodles.

7 Garnish each bowl with the spring onions, and serve with lime wedges.

6 cups (1.4 liters) Vegan Ramen Stock (see page 31)

6 tomatoes, cored and peeled

1 tbsp tomato paste

1 tbsp sugar

1 tbsp white soy sauce

3 tbsp vegetarian red miso paste

2 tsp fermented chili bean paste

24oz (680g) ramen noodles

¼ cup (45g) finely chopped spring onions

1 lime, cut into 4 wedges

# Coconut Curry Tofu Ramen

Coconut milk and curry powder are a wonderful marriage of creamy and sharp flavors. Lime juice is an important addition that highlights and balances the curry. Cilantro finishes this dish with a bold, fresh flavor.

**serves** 4    **prep** 20 min    **cook** 15 min

1   In a large pan over medium heat, bring the stock to a simmer.

2   Add the coconut milk, ginger, salt, curry powder, button mushrooms, red pepper flakes, mirin, white soy sauce, and sugar. Simmer for 5 minutes.

3   Add the tofu, baby spinach, and lime juice. Simmer for 5 minutes.

4   While the broth is simmering, in a large pan of boiling water over high heat, cook the ramen noodles for 4 minutes, stirring occasionally. Drain, rinse, and divide between 4 deep serving bowls.

5   Fill the serving bowls with the hot broth, just covering the noodles.

6   Garnish each bowl with the soft-boiled eggs, spring onions, and cilantro.

6 cups (1.4 liters) Vegan Ramen Stock (see page 31)

½ cup (120ml) coconut milk

1 tsp grated ginger

1 tsp sea salt

2 tsp curry powder

8 button mushrooms, thinly sliced

1 tsp red pepper flakes

2½ tbsp mirin

1 tbsp white soy sauce

1 tsp sugar

1 cup (175g) cubed tofu

1 cup (85g) baby spinach

1½ tbsp lime juice

24oz (680g) ramen noodles

4 soft-boiled eggs, sliced in half lengthwise

¼ cup (45g) finely chopped spring onions

¼ cup (45g) coarsely chopped cilantro

### Make it vegan

Instead of the hard-boiled eggs, top the ramen with another vegetable, such as miso-glazed roasted eggplant.

# Corn Chowder Ramen

Fresh corn is the star of this vegetarian ramen dish. It's enhanced by the salty, complex flavor of the miso. The addition of cream provides a lovely richness to the ramen.

**serves** 4   **prep** 20 min   **cook** 15 min

1   Heat the vegetable oil in a large pan over medium heat. Add the onion, and sauté until translucent. Add the garlic, and sauté for 1 minute, until fragrant.

2   Add the stock, 2 cups (350g) corn, cream, vegetarian white miso paste, mirin, and salt. Simmer for 10 minutes.

3   Using a handheld immersion blender, blend the broth until much of the corn has been incorporated, while still leaving some larger kernel chunks. Add the remaining corn, and simmer for 5 minutes.

4   While the broth is simmering, in a large pan of boiling water over high heat, cook the ramen noodles for 4 minutes, stirring occasionally. Drain, rinse, and divide between 4 deep serving bowls.

5   Fill the bowls with the hot broth, just covering the noodles. Place 1 pat butter in the middle of each bowl, and sprinkle with the chives.

1 tbsp vegetable oil

1 small onion, diced

1 clove garlic, finely chopped

4 cups (1 liter) Vegan Ramen Stock (see page 31)

3 cups (500g) cooked corn kernels

2 cups (500ml) light cream

2½ tbsp vegetarian white miso paste

2 tsp mirin

1 tsp sea salt

24oz (680g) ramen noodles

4 pats butter (about 2 tbsp)

¼ cup (50g) finely chopped chives

## Make it with meat

Add 3oz (85g) cooked, sliced chicken breast atop each bowl.

# Buckwheat Noodle Soup with Enoki and Shiitake

Making your own dashi, or Japanese stock, is a very simple affair that creates a delicate yet flavorful soup base. Here both dried and fresh shiitake are used to make a vegetarian version.

**serves** 4   **prep** 20 min, plus soaking   **cook** 15 min

1 To make the dashi: place the dried kombu, dried shiitake mushrooms, and fresh shiitake mushroom stalks in a saucepan and cover with 4 cups (1.2 liters) cold water. Soak for 1 to 3 hours.

2 After soaking, bring the dashi almost to a boil over medium heat, but remove from the heat just before it boils. Season with salt, and stir in the rice vinegar and soy sauce. Remove and discard the kombu, and let the dashi cool. Strain the dashi through a sieve to remove the shiitake mushrooms.

3 Cook the noodles in boiling, salted water for 3 to 4 minutes until just al dente. Drain and rinse well under cold water.

4 In a large saucepan, bring the dashi to a boil over medium-high heat. Add the enoki mushrooms, spring onions, shiitake mushroom caps, and noodles. Return to a boil until the noodles are heated through and the mushrooms are soft. Remove from the heat and season to taste with salt. Serve immediately, topped with seaweed strips.

10oz (300g) buckwheat soba noodles

1 cup (60g) fresh enoki mushrooms

4 spring onions, thinly sliced on the diagonal

8 small seaweed snack sheets (kim nori), cut into thin strips, to garnish

### For the dashi

3 tbsp (15g) dried kombu, cut into pieces

½oz (15g) dried shiitake mushrooms, about 4

½ cup (60g) fresh shiitake mushrooms, stalks and caps separate, and caps thinly sliced

salt

1 tsp rice vinegar

1 tbsp soy sauce

# Thai Curry, Tomato, and Vegetable Soup with Farro

Tomato soup takes on a whole new life in this recipe, when mixed with Thai curry paste and a variety of fresh vegetables. The addition of farro gives just the right amount of bulk to this satisfying soup.

**serves** 4   **prep** 10 min   **cook** 1 hr 30 min

1   Place the farro in a large, lidded saucepan and cover with water. Place over medium heat, cover, and simmer for about 1 hour or until almost all the water has been absorbed. Drain any remaining water and set aside.

2   Place a large, lidded saucepan over medium heat. Add the coconut milk, stock, tomato paste, Thai red curry paste, and brown sugar and stir to combine. Cover and bring to a boil, stirring occasionally to make sure the ingredients are well combined. Then reduce the heat to a low simmer and cook the soup for a further 20 minutes.

3   Meanwhile, heat the oil in a large frying pan over medium heat. Add the leeks and green pepper and sauté for 10 minutes or until softened and browned in places. Add the zucchini and cook for a further 3 minutes. Remove from the heat and set aside.

4   Add the tomato to the soup. Taste and adjust the seasoning and cook the soup, stirring once, for 5 minutes. Then add the leek mixture and the farro. Stir well to mix and remove from the heat. Ladle the soup into bowls and garnish with cilantro. Serve hot with a green salad and crusty ciabatta bread.

½ cup (75g) uncooked farro

14oz (400g) can light coconut milk

1 cup (200ml) vegetable stock

6oz (175g) can tomato paste

2 tbsp Thai red curry paste

1 tbsp light brown sugar

1 tbsp extra virgin olive oil

2 leeks, white and light green parts only, chopped

1 green pepper, seeded and diced

1 zucchini, diced

1 large beefsteak tomato, diced

salt and freshly ground black pepper

handful cilantro, to garnish

## Make it with fish

Marinate 4 snapper fillets or other firm white fish in 2 tbsp lime juice and 2 tsp sea salt for 30 minutes. Add the fish to the soup in step 4 and gently simmer for 6 to 8 minutes, or until the fish is just cooked through.

# Green Minestrone with Kale and Walnut Pesto

This bright, vibrant soup is made with a variety of fresh spring vegetables that give it a tender-crisp texture. Be sure to add them to the soup in the correct order, so they are all cooked al dente.

**serves** 4-6 **prep** 35 min **cook** 15 min

1 To make the pesto: in a large, nonstick frying pan, toast the walnuts over medium–low heat for 3 to 4 minutes, stirring frequently, until they start to brown. Remove from the heat. Once cool, rub them well in a clean tea towel to remove the skins. Coarsely chop.

2 In a food processor, pulse the walnuts, kale, garlic, lemon juice, basil, olive oil, and 2 tablespoons cold water to form a rough paste. Add the Parmesan and pulse until you reach the desired consistency, adding a little extra olive oil if necessary. The pesto should not be completely smooth. Taste and season with salt and pepper, and pulse once more to combine.

3 Cook the pasta according to the package instructions. Drain and rinse the cooked pasta under cold water. Toss with a drizzle of olive oil to prevent sticking. Set aside.

4 In a large, heavy-bottomed saucepan, heat the olive oil over medium heat. Add the onion, celery, and fennel, and cook for 3 to 4 minutes, stirring occasionally, until soft but not brown. Then add the garlic and cook for 1 minute more.

5 Add the vegetable stock and bring to a boil. Add the green beans and cook for 1 minute. Add the asparagus and peas and cook for 2 minutes more. Finally, add the zucchini and pasta and cook for a final minute. Taste and season with salt and pepper. Serve immediately, with pesto alongside for topping.

4oz (115g) elbow macaroni or orzo

2 tbsp olive oil, plus extra to toss

1 small yellow onion, finely diced

1 celery stalk, finely diced

⅓ large fennel bulb, finely diced

1 large clove garlic, finely chopped

6 cups (1.4 liters) vegetable stock

large handful young green beans, finely sliced

10 asparagus spears, finely sliced

½ cup (60g) frozen peas

½ small zucchini, halved lengthwise and finely sliced

### For the pesto
⅔ cup (60g) walnut halves

½ cup (30g) washed, deveined, and shredded young kale

1 large clove garlic, crushed

2 tbsp lemon juice

12 leaves basil

4 tbsp olive oil

2 tbsp grated Parmesan cheese

salt and freshly ground black pepper

### Make it vegan

Use a plant-based Parmesan cheese or nutritional yeast instead of Parmesan cheese, and ensure the pasta is eggless.

# Creamy Spinach and Mung Bean Soup

Don't let the bright color fool you—this soup is as luxurious as it is good for you, and especially tasty with freshly baked bread.

**serves** 4   **prep** 25 min   **cook** 40 min

1   In a fire-resistant casserole dish or stock pot, melt the butter over medium heat. Add the onion and cook for 3-4 minutes until translucent. Add the garlic and cook for 2 minutes.

2   Add the potato and stir to combine. Cook for 2-3 minutes. Add 2 cups (500ml) stock and bring to a boil. Reduce the heat to a simmer and cook, covered, for 12-15 minutes, until the potatoes are tender.

3   Add the spinach and mung beans and cook for an additional 5 minutes, or until the spinach wilts and the mung beans are warmed through. Leave to cool.

4   With a blender (working in batches) or a handheld blender, puree the soup until smooth. Return the pureed mixture to the pan and stir in the sherry, cayenne, and nutmeg. For a thinner consistency, add some of the remaining stock as desired. Season with salt and pepper to taste.

5   Reheat the soup over medium heat. Transfer to serving bowls and top with Parmesan. Serve immediately.

- 1 tbsp unsalted butter
- 1 medium onion, diced
- 1 clove garlic, finely chopped
- 1 medium russet potato, peeled and cut into ½in (1cm) chunks
- 3 cups (750ml) vegetable stock
- 6oz (175g) bag baby spinach
- 1 cup (175g) cooked mung beans
- 2 tbsp dry sherry
- ⅛ tsp ground cayenne pepper
- ⅛ tsp ground nutmeg
- salt and freshly ground black pepper
- ¼ cup (20g) grated Parmesan cheese

## Why not try ...

Garnish with flat-leaf parsley or watercress for a more pronounced green flavor.

### Make it vegan

Replace the butter with an equal amount of coconut oil, and use a plant-based Parmesan cheese.

### Make it with meat

Crumble 1 tbsp crisped prosciutto on top of each bowl of soup.

# Pigeon Pea and Pumpkin Chili

Pumpkin may seem like an unusual ingredient in chili, but its sweetness is a lovely complement to the spiciness of this soup.

**serves** 6   **prep** 25 min   **cook** 45 min

1   In a large stock pot, heat the oil over medium-low heat. Add the onion and cook for 2–3 minutes until soft. Add the garlic and jalapeño and cook for an additional minute.

2   Incorporate the tomatoes, cumin, and chipotle chili powder. Stir in the stock, bring to a boil, reduce the heat and then simmer for 5 minutes. Stir in the pigeon peas (or black-eyed peas), adzuki beans, and corn. Return to a boil then reduce the heat to low and simmer, covered, for 20 minutes.

3   Fold in the pumpkin and stir to combine. Cook, covered, for another 10 minutes. Season with salt and pepper to taste. Transfer to 6 serving bowls, garnish with the chopped cilantro, and serve immediately.

1 tbsp olive oil

1 small yellow onion, diced

2 cloves garlic, finely chopped

1 small jalapeño, seeded and minced

14oz (400g) can diced tomatoes

2½ tsp ground cumin

1½ tsp chipotle chili powder

2 cups (500ml) vegetable stock

2½ cups (375g) cooked pigeon peas or black-eyed peas

2 cups (400g) cooked adzuki beans

1 cup (115g) corn kernels

15oz (425g) can pure pumpkin

salt and freshly ground black pepper

¾ cup (60g) chopped cilantro, to garnish

## Make it with meat

Cook ½ pound (225g) ground turkey along with the onion in step 1.

# Chickpea and Navy Bean Bisque

While not a traditional bisque, this soup certainly seems like one with its silky, rich texture. This simple, elegant recipe makes an excellent first course for a dinner party.

**serves** 4   **prep** 15 min   **cook** 30 min

1  In a fire-resistant casserole dish or large saucepan, warm the oil over medium-low heat until shimmering. Add the leek and cook for 4–5 minutes until soft and translucent. Add the garlic and cook for an additional 2 minutes.

2  Add the vermouth and cook for 1–2 minutes. Incorporate the stock, navy beans, and chickpeas. Bring to a boil, then reduce to a simmer and cook, covered, for 15 minutes. Remove from the heat and leave to cool for 5–10 minutes.

3  Transfer the mixture to a blender and puree until smooth. Return to the pan over medium heat, stir in the cream, and heat. Season with salt and pepper to taste. Transfer to serving bowls, garnish with the hazelnuts and a swirl of oil, and serve immediately.

1½ tsp olive oil, plus extra
   to garnish

1 leek, white parts only, sliced

1 clove garlic, finely chopped

1 tbsp dry vermouth

3 cups (750ml) vegetable stock

2 cups (450g) cooked navy beans

1 cup (175g) cooked chickpeas

¼ cup (60ml) heavy cream

salt and freshly ground black pepper

chopped toasted hazelnuts,
   to garnish

### Make it vegan

The cooked chickpeas are naturally creamy, so you can easily omit the heavy cream for a vegan-friendly version

# Brazilian Black Bean and Pumpkin Stew

A colorful and gutsy dish, you could always add some spicy sausage or chorizo if you prefer a meaty meal. Black beans are also called turtle beans and need soaking overnight.

**serves** 4-6   **prep** 25 min, plus soaking   **cook** 2½-3 hr

1  Preheat the oven to 325°F (160°C). Put the beans in a large heavy-bottomed pan and cover with water. Bring to a boil, then reduce to a simmer, partially cover with the lid, and cook on low heat for 1 hour. Drain and set aside.

2  Heat the oil in a large heavy-bottomed pan over medium heat, add the onion, and cook for 3-4 minutes until soft. Season with salt and pepper, stir in the garlic, and cook for 1-2 minutes until soft. Stir in the pumpkin or butternut squash, red peppers, tomatoes, and chile.

3  Add the beans, pour over the stock, and bring to a boil. Then reduce to a simmer, cover with the lid and put in the oven for 1½-2 hours. Taste and season, if necessary, then stir in the mango and cilantro. Serve with some sour cream and rice on the side.

1½ cups (325g) dried black beans, soaked overnight and drained

1 tbsp olive oil

1 onion, finely chopped

salt and freshly ground black pepper

3 cloves garlic, finely chopped

1 small pumpkin or butternut squash, peeled, seeded, and diced

2 red peppers, seeded and diced

2 (14oz/400g) cans diced tomatoes

1 small green chile, seeded and diced

3 cups (900ml) hot vegetable stock

1 mango, peeled, stone removed, and diced

bunch cilantro, chopped

## Make it with meat

Add 9oz (250g) chopped spicy sausage or chorizo to the pan in step 2 after adding the garlic. Cook for 6-8 minutes until seared.

# Kitchari Stew with Kamut

The word "kitchari" literally means mixture, and is an Indian recipe that mixes two or more grains for a soothing and warming dish. This recipe uses kamut instead of rice, for more texture and bite.

**serves** 3  **prep** 10 min, plus overnight soaking  **cook** 2 hr 10 min

1 Place the peas in a large bowl, cover with water, and leave to soak for about 12 hours. Place the kamut in a separate bowl, cover with water, and leave to soak overnight or for up to 8 hours. Drain any remaining water from the peas and kamut. Rinse under running water, drain well, and set aside.

2 Heat the oil in a large, lidded saucepan over medium heat. Add the ginger, turmeric, cumin, coriander, and cinnamon. Reduce the heat to low and cook for 1–2 minutes, stirring frequently, making sure the spices do not burn.

3 Add the peas, kamut, and water to the pan. Season with salt and bring the mixture to a simmer. Cover partially and cook, stirring occasionally, for 2 hours or until the peas have broken down and the kamut is tender and chewy. Taste and adjust the seasoning, if needed. Remove from the heat and garnish with cilantro. Serve hot.

¾ cup (150g) yellow split peas

½ cup (100g) uncooked kamut

1 tbsp coconut oil or ghee

2in (5cm) piece fresh ginger, finely chopped

2 tsp ground turmeric

2 tsp ground cumin

1 tsp ground coriander

½ tsp ground cinnamon

6 cups (1.5 liters) water

salt

handful cilantro, to garnish

## Why not try ...

If you can't find kamut, stick with the traditional version of this dish and use basmati rice. Add ½ cup (100g) rinsed basmati rice with the soaked peas and water in step 3. You should only need to simmer for 1 hour, stirring periodically as the rice may stick to the bottom of the pan.

# Red Wine–Braised Beets and Lentils with Farro

Beets and lentils are a match made in heaven when braised in a full-bodied red wine. Be sure to use a wine of good quality, as it will enhance the flavor of the stew and you can save a glass to have with your meal.

**serves** 4   **prep** 30 min, plus overnight soaking and chilling   **cook** 1 hr 20 min

1   Place the farro in a large bowl, cover with water, and leave to soak overnight or for up to 12 hours. Then drain and rinse under running water. Drain well.

2   Heat 1 tablespoon of the light olive oil in a saucepan over medium heat. Add the farro and sliced garlic. Season to taste with salt and cook for 5 minutes, stirring occasionally, until the farro is lightly toasted. Add 4 cups (900ml) of water and bring to a boil. Then reduce the heat to a simmer, cover, and cook for 25–30 minutes or until the farro is tender. Drain any remaining water and rinse under running water. Drain well and set aside.

3   For the lentils and vegetables, heat the remaining light olive oil in a large, heavy-bottomed, lidded saucepan over medium heat. Add the onion and cook for 2–3 minutes or until softened. Then add the garlic, beets, and carrots. Season to taste with a good grinding of pepper and cook for 5–10 minutes, stirring occasionally. Add the tomato paste in a corner of the pan, cook for 1–2 minutes, then stir to mix with the vegetables.

4   Add the lentils, wine, stock, rosemary, thyme, and bay leaf. Bring to a boil. Then reduce the heat to a simmer and cook, covered, for 25 minutes or until the lentils and vegetables are cooked through. Season with salt and cook for a further 5–10 minutes. Remove from the heat and discard the rosemary, thyme, and bay leaf.

5   Place the yogurt, lemon juice, lemon zest, crushed garlic, and extra virgin olive oil in a bowl. Finely chop the parsley and add to the bowl. Season with a pinch of salt and whisk to combine. Cover with plastic wrap and chill for 15 minutes. To serve, divide the farro between four serving plates, top with the beets and lentils, and spoon over a dollop of yogurt.

¾ cup (150g) uncooked farro

3 tbsp light olive oil

1 clove garlic, sliced

salt and freshly ground black pepper

1 cup (250g) Greek yogurt

1 tbsp lemon juice

1 tsp lemon zest

1 small clove garlic, crushed

1 tbsp extra virgin olive oil

handful flat-leaf parsley

**For the lentils and vegetables**

1 onion, finely sliced

3 cloves garlic, crushed

3 large beets, peeled and diced into 1in (3cm) cubes

2 carrots, chopped into 1in (2.5cm) pieces

2 tsp tomato paste

½ cup (100g) black beluga lentils, rinsed and cleaned

¾ cup (200ml) good-quality red wine

1 cup (250ml) vegetable stock

sprig each rosemary and thyme

1 bay leaf

**Make it vegan**

Use a vegan yogurt alternative, such as coconut yogurt (see page 38), rather than Greek yogurt.

# Curries and Stir-Fries

Curries and stir-fries are ideal flexitarian meals. From green lentil curry to quinoa cashew stir-fry and crispy fried tofu, these dishes are nutritious and full of flavor on their own, or simple to add dairy or meat to.

# Chickpea Tikka Masala in Lettuce Cups

Creamy and surprisingly mild, the curry flavor in this dish is a wonderful match for the slightly sweet butter lettuce and the textured chickpeas.

**serves** 6 **prep** 20 min **cook** 30 min

1 In a large frying pan, heat the ghee over medium-low heat until shimmering. Add the white onion and cook for 2 minutes, or until soft. Add the garam masala, turmeric, chile, and ginger. Cook for an additional minute to warm the spices.

2 Stir in the chickpeas, tomato puree, and yogurt. Bring to a boil then reduce the heat to low and cook for 20 minutes, or until the sauce and chickpeas are completely warmed through. Season with salt and pepper to taste. Remove from the heat and let sit for 5 minutes.

3 To assemble, divide the chickpea mixture evenly among the lettuce leaves. Garnish with the red onion and cilantro and serve immediately.

1 tbsp ghee

1 small white onion, chopped

1 tbsp garam masala

½ tsp turmeric

1 small green chile, seeded and finely chopped

¼ tsp grated fresh ginger

2½ cups (350g) cooked chickpeas

2 cups (500ml) tomato puree

¼ cup (50g) plain Greek yogurt

salt and freshly ground black pepper

12 leaves butter lettuce, washed and dried

¼ cup (60g) thinly sliced red onion

2 tbsp chopped cilantro

## Why not try ...

For texture and crunch, use Savoy cabbage instead of the lettuce.

### Make it vegan

Replace the ghee with canola oil and the yogurt with coconut yogurt (see page 38).

### Make it with meat

Add 4½oz (125g) cooked, chopped chicken breast along with the chickpeas in step 2.

# Black Sesame and Coconut Curry Bowl

By themselves, shirataki noodles have very little taste, so pan-frying them in the curry sauce allows them to absorb all the gently spiced flavors of this simple vegan dish.

**serves** 4   **prep** 10 min   **cook** 25 min

1  In a medium, heavy-bottomed saucepan, melt 2 tablespoons coconut oil over medium heat. Add the onion and cook for 2 to 3 minutes until soft but not brown. Incorporate the garlic and ginger and cook for 1 minute more.

2  Add the red pepper and mushrooms and cook for 2 to 3 minutes until they start to deepen in color. Add the remaining 1 tablespoon coconut oil, curry powder, and chili powder (if using), and stir well to combine. Reduce the heat to low and cook for 1 minute until the spices release fragrance.

3  Incorporate the coconut milk and vegetable stock. Add the sweet potatoes and bring to a boil. Reduce to a simmer and cook, uncovered, for 10 to 12 minutes until the sweet potatoes are soft.

4  Meanwhile, bring a pan of water to a boil. Transfer the shirataki noodles to a colander and rinse thoroughly under cold running water for at least 30 seconds to rinse off the packaging liquid. In the pan of boiling water, cook the noodles for 2 minutes. Drain well, and set aside to cool completely.

5  Heat a large, nonstick frying pan over a high heat. Once cool, dry-fry the noodles for 2 minutes, stirring constantly. Add most of the sauce to the noodles and cook for another 2 minutes until the sauce is mostly absorbed.

6  Divide the noodles among 4 serving bowls and top with equal amounts of the curried vegetables and the remaining sauce. Garnish with equal amounts of the cilantro, spring onions, and sesame seeds, and serve immediately.

3 tbsp coconut oil

½ red onion, finely chopped

2 cloves garlic, finely chopped

1in (2.5cm) piece fresh ginger, finely chopped

½ large red pepper, diced

2 cups (150g) mushrooms, peeled and quartered

2 tsp curry powder

¼ tsp chili powder (optional)

14oz (400ml) can coconut milk

½ cup (120ml) vegetable stock

2¼ cups (10oz) peeled and diced (½in/1cm cubes) sweet potato

2 (7oz/200g) packages shirataki or vermicelli noodles

handful cilantro

2 spring onions, trimmed and sliced on the diagonal

½ tsp black sesame seeds

## Make it with fish

Top each bowl with 4 cooked shrimp before you serve.

# Lentil and Broccoli Green Curry

The crunch of broccoli complements the creamy curry sauce, and the lentils introduce another layer of texture to this Thai dish, which is perfect over brown basmati or jasmine rice.

**serves** 8   **prep** 30 min   **cook** 35 min

1  In a large saucepan, warm the oil over medium-low heat until shimmering. Add the shallot and garlic and cook for 2 minutes, or until soft. Add the curry paste and stir to combine. Cook for an additional minute.

2  Add the coconut milk, soy sauce, and lime leaf or lime juice. Simmer for 10 minutes. Add the red pepper and cook for another 10 minutes, or until the pepper starts to become tender.

3  Stir in the broccoli, lentils, mushrooms, green beans, and basil. Cook for an additional 5-10 minutes, until the green beans and broccoli are tender and the mushrooms are cooked. Remove the lime leaf, if using. Season with salt and pepper to taste. Serve immediately.

1 tbsp vegetable oil

1 shallot, finely chopped

1 clove garlic, finely chopped

1 tbsp green curry paste

14oz (400ml) can coconut milk

1½ tsp soy sauce

1 lime leaf or 1 tbsp fresh lime juice

1 small red pepper, seeded and julienned

3 cups (200g) broccoli florets

1 cup (325g) cooked green lentils

1 cup (100g) sliced shiitake mushrooms

⅔ cup (75g) chopped fresh green beans

1 tbsp finely chopped basil

salt and freshly ground black pepper

## Make it with meat

Add 8oz (225g) sliced raw chicken breast, and cook with the shallots and garlic in step 1.

# Thai Yellow Pumpkin Curry with Quinoa

This vibrant curry with its fresh, Thai flavors uses pumpkin and quinoa to create a hearty and warming supper that is comforting in fall or winter.

**serves** 4–6   **prep** 10 min   **cook** 40 min

1  Heat the oil in a large, lidded saucepan over medium heat. Add the curry paste and onions and cook for 2 minutes, stirring frequently. Then add the pumpkin, coconut milk, stock, and quinoa to the pan. Bring to a simmer, cover, and cook for about 30 minutes.

2  Add the chickpeas and cook for 5 minutes or until the pumpkin is tender. Taste and adjust the seasoning as necessary. Remove from the heat. Garnish with cilantro and serve immediately with lime wedges.

1 tbsp coconut oil or sunflower oil

3 tbsp Thai yellow curry paste

1 onion, finely chopped

1 pumpkin, about 1¾lb (800g), seeded and chopped into bite-size pieces

14oz (400ml) can coconut milk

1¼ cups (300ml) vegetable stock

1 cup (200g) uncooked quinoa

14oz (400g) can chickpeas, drained

salt and freshly ground black pepper

4 tbsp chopped cilantro, to garnish

2 limes, cut into wedges

## Why not try ...

You could try using sweet potato in place of the pumpkin, and garnish with flat-leaf parsley instead of the cilantro.

# Pigeon Pea Vindaloo

Characteristic of vindaloo, the high heat level in this Indian curry balances with warm spices, such as cinnamon and cardamom. Serve with rice or naan and some cooling yogurt raita.

**serves** 4   **prep** 25 min   **cook** 35 min

1  In a small bowl, combine the cumin, coriander, turmeric, cardamom, mustard seeds, and paprika and stir thoroughly to combine.

2  In a heavy-bottomed pan, heat the oil over medium heat until shimmering. Add the onion and cook for 3–4 minutes until it starts to become translucent.

3  Stir in the garlic, ginger, and chile, and cook for an additional 2 minutes. Incorporate the spice mixture, bay leaf, cinnamon stick, tomato puree, vinegar, and water, and bring to a boil. Reduce the heat and simmer, covered, for 10 minutes.

4  Add the pigeon peas (or black-eyed peas) and stir to combine. Bring to a boil then reduce to a simmer and cook, covered, for 20 minutes. Remove the cinnamon stick and bay leaf. Season with salt and pepper to taste. Serve immediately.

3¾ tsp ground cumin

1 tbsp ground coriander

¾ tsp turmeric

⅔ tsp ground cardamom

1½ tsp ground mustard seeds

1 tbsp paprika

1 tbsp vegetable oil

1 small onion, diced

3 cloves garlic, finely chopped

2¼ tsp finely chopped fresh ginger

1 large hot red chile, seeded and finely chopped

1 bay leaf

1 cinnamon stick

1 cup (225g) tomato puree

1 tbsp red wine vinegar

1 cup (240ml) water

3 cups (450g) cooked pigeon peas or black-eyed peas

salt and freshly ground black pepper

## Make it with meat

Brown 1lb (450g) cubed beef chuck and add with the tomato puree.

# Braised Chickpeas with Preserved Lemon

A North African condiment, these lemon slices preserved in brine add a fragrant touch to a simply braised chickpea and chard recipe.

**serves** 6   **prep** 15 min   **cook** 35 min

1   In a large fire-resistant casserole dish, warm the oil over medium heat until shimmering. Add the onion and cook for 2 minutes, or until soft. Add the garlic and cook for an additional minute.

2   Add the chickpeas and Swiss chard and stir to combine. Add the stock and cook, covered, for 15 minutes, or until the chard begins to wilt.

3   Stir in the olives and preserved lemon. Cook, covered, for an additional 10 minutes. Season with salt and pepper to taste. Serve immediately.

1 tbsp olive oil

1 small onion, chopped

1 clove garlic, finely chopped

3 cups (500g) cooked chickpeas

1lb (450g) chopped Swiss chard, leaves and stems

½ cup (120ml) vegetable stock

½ cup (75g) chopped green olives

1½ tsp finely chopped preserved lemon, or zest and juice of 1 lemon

salt and freshly ground black pepper

### Make it with meat

Finely dice 2oz (60g) pancetta and cook with the onion in step 1.

# Cauliflower Curry

For this recipe, potatoes and cauliflower are tumbled in a tikka coconut sauce. This is a simple and economical dish to make, and can easily be made ahead and reheated when required.

**serves** 4–6   **prep** 15 min   **cook** 1 hr

1  Heat the oil in a large heavy-bottomed pan over medium heat, add the onion, and cook for 3–4 minutes until soft. Season with salt and pepper, stir in the ginger, garlic, and chiles, and cook for a couple of minutes. Stir in the tikka paste, chickpeas, coconut milk, and stock and bring to a boil. Reduce to a simmer and cook gently, partially covered with the lid and stirring occasionally, for 30 minutes.

2  Meanwhile, bring another large pan of salted water to a boil. Add the potatoes and cook for about 15 minutes or until just beginning to soften. Remove the potatoes with a slotted spoon and set aside. Put the cauliflower in the boiling water and cook for about 5 minutes, then drain well.

3  Add the potato and cauliflower into the sauce and turn so they are well coated, then simmer very gently for a further 15 minutes or so, to allow all the flavors to mingle. Serve with some rice and naan.

1 tbsp vegetable oil

1 onion, coarsely chopped

salt and freshly ground black pepper

2in (5cm) piece fresh ginger, peeled and finely chopped

3 cloves garlic, finely chopped

2 green chiles, seeded and finely chopped

2 tbsp medium-hot tikka curry paste

15oz (400g) can chickpeas, drained and rinsed

14oz (400ml) can coconut milk

2½ cups (600ml) hot vegetable stock

3 potatoes, peeled and cut into bite-size pieces

1 cauliflower, cut into bite-size florets

# Paneer and Sweet Pepper Curry

The sweet peppers marry well with the paneer in this mild vegetarian curry. Paneer is an Indian cheese that won't melt upon cooking; you'll find it with the other cheeses at the supermarket.

**serves** 4-6  **prep** 20 min  **cook** 1 hr

1   Heat half the oil in a heavy-bottomed pan over medium-high heat, add the paneer and cook for 5-8 minutes, stirring, until golden all over. Remove and set aside.

2   Heat the remaining oil in the pan, add the ginger, chiles, curry leaves, cumin seeds, garam masala, and turmeric, and stir well to coat with the oil. Then add the red peppers and cook over low heat for about 15 minutes until beginning to soften.

3   Add the tomatoes and ½ cup (100ml) water and cook on low for 15 minutes. Return the paneer to the pan, season with salt and pepper, then simmer gently for 15-20 minutes, topping up with a little hot water if needed. Stir in the cilantro and serve with rice, chapatis, or naan.

2 tbsp vegetable oil

8oz (230g) package paneer, cubed

4in (10cm) piece fresh ginger, peeled and sliced

2 red chiles, seeded and finely chopped

2 tbsp crushed dried curry leaves

2 tsp cumin seeds

4 tsp garam masala

2 tsp ground turmeric

6 red peppers, seeded and sliced

6 tomatoes, peeled and roughly chopped

salt and freshly ground black pepper

bunch cilantro, finely chopped

## Make it vegan

Replace the paneer with the same amount of cubed firm tofu, and follow the same instructions in steps 1 and 3.

# Zucchini, Herb, and Lemon Tagine

Light, fresh, and zingy, this vegetarian version of a tagine is full of punchy flavors. It is a good dish to prepare ahead as the flavors improve with reheating.

**serves** 4   **prep** 25 min   **cook** 45–55 min

1  Heat half the oil in a large heavy-bottomed pan or tagine over low heat, add the onions, and cook for 8 minutes until soft and translucent. Season well with salt and pepper, then stir in the garlic, fennel seeds, cinnamon, harissa, and preserved lemons.

2  Add the tomatoes and stir well, crushing them with the back of a wooden spoon. Bring to a boil, then reduce to a simmer and cook over low heat for 30–40 minutes. If the sauce starts to dry out, top up with a little hot water.

3  Cook the broccoli in a pan of boiling salted water for 3–5 minutes or until tender, then drain and refresh in cold water. Drain again and set aside. Heat the remaining oil in a frying pan over low heat, add the zucchini, season with salt and pepper, and cook, stirring frequently, for 5 minutes or until it starts to color a little. Add the lemon juice and stir in the dill. Add the broccoli and zucchini to the sauce and stir in the parsley. Serve on warmed plates with couscous, lemon wedges, and a spoonful of harissa on the side.

2 tbsp olive oil

1 red onion, finely chopped

salt and freshly ground black pepper

3 cloves garlic, finely chopped

pinch fennel seeds

pinch ground cinnamon

1–2 tsp harissa paste, plus extra to serve

2 preserved lemons, quartered and flesh discarded

14oz (400g) can whole tomatoes, chopped

1 head broccoli, broken into florets

3 zucchini, trimmed and sliced

juice of 1 lemon

handful dill, finely chopped

handful flat-leaf parsley, finely chopped

# Miso Japanese Eggplant and Buckwheat Noodles

Japanese eggplants are long, thin, and have very few seeds, but you can also use any young eggplants you can find. With its umami flavor, this dish tastes light while being filling.

**serves** 4   **prep** 15 min   **cook** 30 min

1   Preheat the oven to 425°F (220°C). Lightly score the cut side of the eggplant with the tip of a sharp knife to make a crisscross design. Place cut side down on a lightly oiled baking sheet and transfer to the top rack of the oven. Bake for 10 to 15 minutes until soft.

2   Meanwhile, bring a large pan of salted water to a boil. To make the glaze: in a small saucepan, whisk together the miso paste and 4 tablespoons hot water. Then whisk in the mirin, sugar, and sesame oil. Bring briefly to a boil, whisking constantly until the sugar has dissolved. Remove from the heat and set aside.

3   Cook the noodles in the boiling water according to the package instructions until just al dente, then drain and rinse briefly under cold water. Toss with a drizzle of sesame oil to prevent sticking.

4   When the eggplant is soft, remove from the oven and turn the broiler on high. Line a baking sheet with foil and arrange the eggplant cut side up on the sheet. Brush the cut sides with the glaze. Return to the top rack of the oven and broil until well browned and crisp on top, about 10 minutes. Remove the eggplant from the oven occasionally to brush with more glaze when it has been absorbed (about 3 times). Sprinkle with the sesame seeds and broil one last time until the sesame seeds are brown.

5   Heat the sunflower oil in a wok over medium heat. Add the cabbage and bean sprouts and stir-fry for 1 minute. Stir the soy sauce into the remaining glaze. Add the noodles, spring onions, and glaze to the wok and cook for 1 minute until heated through. Add the chopped cilantro and toss well to combine. Divide among 4 serving dishes, and top each with 2 pieces of eggplant. Garnish with cilantro and serve immediately.

2 firm Japanese or other young eggplants, trimmed and halved lengthwise, then in half widthwise

salt

8oz (225g) buckwheat soba noodles

sesame oil, to toss

1 tbsp sesame seeds

1 tbsp sunflower oil, plus extra for greasing

2½ cups (175g) shredded green cabbage

1½ cups (175g) bean sprouts

1 tbsp soy sauce

4 large spring onions, trimmed and very finely sliced

2 tbsp chopped cilantro, plus whole leaves to garnish

### For the glaze
2 tbsp white miso paste

4 tbsp mirin

4½ tsp sugar

2 tsp sesame oil

## Make it with fish

Add 14oz (400g) skinned, cubed salmon to the wok in step 5 before the cabbage, and cook for 2–3 minutes.

# Quinoa Cashew Stir-Fry with Chile and Lime Sauce

This simple stir-fry is light, yet full of flavor and color. The lime gives it an added zing that pairs well with the sweetness of the toasted cashews and crunchy vegetables.

**serves** 2  **prep** 20 min  **cook** 20 min

1 Place the quinoa in a large saucepan. Cover with ½ cup (125ml) of water and simmer for about 10 minutes or until all the water has been absorbed. Then remove from the heat and set aside.

2 Heat a large wok or frying pan over high heat. Add the cashews and toast until lightly colored. Remove from the heat and coarsely chop. Add the oil to the pan. Then add the carrots, cabbage, bean sprouts, and onions. Cook, stirring frequently, for about 5 minutes or until lightly cooked.

3 Meanwhile, for the sauce, place all the ingredients in a bowl and mix to combine. Add the quinoa to the vegetables and mix well. Pour over the chile and lime sauce, mix well, and cook for 1–2 minutes. Remove from the heat and serve hot.

½ cup (100g) uncooked quinoa

½ cup (50g) cashews

2 tbsp light olive oil

1 cup (115g) carrot, coarsely chopped

1½ cups (115g) cabbage, coarsely chopped

1 cup (100g) bean sprouts

¾ cup (85g) red onion, thinly sliced

### For the sauce

juice of 1 lime and grated zest of ½ lime

2 tbsp soy sauce

2 tbsp honey

1 red chile, seeded and finely chopped

### Make it with meat

Cut 7oz (200g) chicken breast into slices and cook with the vegetables in step 2.

# Poblanos Stuffed with Spicy Sorghum and Black Bean Stir-Fry

Green poblano peppers have a sweet and mild heat that makes them the perfect companion for this well-spiced sorghum stir-fry. An impressive dish, it's also easy to make.

**serves** 6   **prep** 10 min, plus cooling   **cook** 1 hr 20 min

1  Place the sorghum and stock in a small, lidded saucepan and bring to a boil. Then reduce to a simmer, cover, and cook for about 45 minutes. Remove from the heat and leave, covered, for a further 10 minutes. Then drain any remaining liquid and set aside.

2  Meanwhile, preheat the oven to 450°F (230°C). Place the poblano peppers on a lined baking sheet. Brush with half of the oil and season with salt and pepper. Place in the oven and roast for 15–20 minutes, until they start to brown and are tender. Remove from the heat and leave to cool slightly. Once cool enough to handle, slit the peppers in the center, lengthwise, and remove the seeds.

3  Heat the remaining oil in a large cast-iron pan over medium heat. Add the onions and sauté for 5–8 minutes or until softened. Then add the garlic, chili powder, oregano, cumin, and cayenne pepper. Mix to combine and cook for 2–3 minutes, stirring frequently.

4  Add the sorghum, beans, and tomatoes and stir to combine. Cook for 5 minutes, stirring occasionally. Then add the corn and cook for a further 2–3 minutes. Taste, and adjust the seasoning if needed. Spoon the stir-fry mixture into the poblano peppers and scatter any extra on the plates. Garnish with Cheddar and serve immediately.

½ cup (100g) uncooked sorghum (found in health food or African food stores)

2 cups (500ml) vegetable stock

6 large poblano peppers

2 tbsp sunflower oil

salt and freshly ground black pepper

1 small red onion, coarsely chopped

3 cloves garlic, crushed

1 tsp chili powder

1 tsp oregano

½ tsp ground cumin

¼ tsp cayenne pepper

14oz (400g) can black beans, drained and rinsed

1 cup (150g) plum tomatoes, seeded and diced

½ cup (150g) canned corn kernels

1 tbsp freshly grated Cheddar cheese, to serve

## Make it vegan

Use a plant-based cheese alternative or nut cheese (see page 37) instead of Cheddar.

# Sesame-Crusted Tofu with Green Beans and Black Rice

This vegetarian dish uses sesame seeds in place of breadcrumbs to coat tender tofu—giving it a crunchy, nutty texture—and pairs it with a spicy, salty green bean stir-fry.

**serves** 4   **prep** 15 min   **cook** 50 min

1  Place the rice in a large saucepan and cook according to package instructions. Remove from the heat, cover, and set aside. Pat the tofu dry with paper towel and cut 16 (1in-/2.5cm-) thick triangles. Set aside.

2  Place the cornstarch and sesame seeds in a shallow dish and mix to combine. Place the egg in a small bowl. Season the tofu with salt and pepper and brush lightly with the egg. Then toss the tofu in the cornstarch mixture until lightly coated.

3  Heat the grape-seed oil in a large frying pan over medium-low heat. Once the oil has heated, reduce the heat to low and add the tofu. Cook for 3–4 minutes on each side, turning the tofu gently to prevent it breaking apart,until evenly browned on each side. Remove with a slotted spoon, set aside on a lined plate, and keep warm. Drain the excess oil from the pan.

4  Add the sesame oil to the pan and increase the heat to medium. Add the onions, ginger, and chiles. Cook for about 5 minutes, stirring frequently, until softened. Then add the garlic and cook for another minute. Add the green beans and cook, stirring, for 3–4 minutes.

5  Add the tamari sauce and spring onions. Season with pepper and cook, stirring, for about 3 minutes. Add the tofu and gently heat through for 2 minutes. Do not stir the tofu as it may break apart. Remove from the heat. Divide the rice between four serving plates. Top with the green bean and onion stir-fry and the tofu. Sprinkle over sesame seeds, drizzle with some oil and tamari sauce, and serve warm.

1⅔ cups (300g) black rice

14oz (400g) extra firm tofu, drained

4 tbsp cornstarch

4 tbsp sesame seeds, plus extra to serve

1 egg, lightly beaten

salt and freshly ground black pepper

2–3 tbsp grape-seed oil

2 tbsp sesame oil, plus extra to serve

1 onion, thinly sliced

1 tsp grated fresh ginger

3 mild red chiles, seeded and sliced into ½in (1cm) pieces

3 cloves garlic, crushed and thinly sliced

2 cups (200g) green beans, blanched

1 tbsp tamari sauce, plus extra to serve

2 spring onions, cut into 1in (2.5cm) long pieces

## Make it vegan

Use 3 tbsp aquafaba in place of the egg. Lightly beat it with a whisk and use it as you would the egg in step 2.

# Baked Dishes
# and Casseroles

Satisfy your craving for hearty meals with these casseroles
and baked dishes. From lasagna to enchiladas,
you'll find easy weeknight dinners to enjoy
when the weather starts to cool.

# Creamy Fontina and Truffle Lasagna

The sweet, creamy fontina and truffle oil make this an especially luxurious lasagna. The buttery sauce is delicious with a sharp green salad to balance the richness of the dish.

**serves** 6  **prep** 20 min  **cook** 1 hr, plus standing

1   Preheat the oven to 400°F (200°C). To make the filling: in a large frying pan, heat the olive oil over high heat. Working in two batches, partially cook the mushrooms for 3 to 4 minutes, turning often. Recombine the batches and add the garlic. Cook for 1 minute more.

2   Add the artichokes and truffle oil. Season well with salt and pepper. Stir, then set aside to cool.

3   To make the sauce: in a heavy-bottomed saucepan, melt the butter over medium heat. Remove from the heat and whisk in the rice flour. Gradually whisk in the milk. Return the pan to the heat and cook, whisking constantly, for 2 to 3 minutes until the mixture thickens and starts to boil. Reduce the heat to low and continue to cook for 2 to 3 minutes, whisking occasionally. Finally, add two-thirds of the cheese, and whisk until melted. Remove from the heat and season well with salt and pepper.

4   To assemble the lasagna: in a 9×13in (23×33cm) baking dish, spread one-quarter of the sauce to coat the bottom of the dish. On top of that, layer one-third of the filling, and a single layer of lasagna sheets. Then layer with another one-quarter of the sauce, one-third of the filling, and a single layer of lasagna sheets. Top with another one-quarter of the sauce, the remaining filling, and a final layer of lasagna sheets.

5   Cover the top with the remaining sauce and remaining cheese. Transfer to the middle rack of the oven and bake for 40 to 45 minutes until well browned and cooked through. Leave to stand for 10 to 15 minutes before cutting and serving.

2 tbsp olive oil

1lb (450g) cleaned, trimmed, and coarsely chopped mixed mushrooms (such as cremini, portobello, oyster, and shiitake)

1 large clove garlic, crushed

12oz (340g) jar grilled artichoke halves in oil, drained and coarsely chopped

2 tsp truffle oil

salt and freshly ground black pepper

8–10 fresh lasagna sheets (see p33)

**For the sauce**

4 tbsp (60g) unsalted butter

⅓ cup (60g) sweet white rice flour

2⅓ cups (550ml) whole milk

1 cup (140g) fontina cheese (or mozzarella), coarsely grated

## Make it vegan

Replace the sauce in this recipe with vegan Béchamel Sauce (see page 42). Top the lasagna with a plant-based mozzarella in step 5.

# Curried Black Lentil Stuffed Onions

The nuttiness of black lentils and quinoa mixed with creamy goat cheese makes these onions a unique main course.

**serves** 8  **prep** 30 min  **cook** 1 hr

1 Preheat the oven to 375°F (190°C). Trim both ends off the onions and discard the skins. Cut each onion horizontally in half to create two flat sections. To create a well for the filling, with a spoon or melon baller gently scoop out the middle of each onion half, leaving the bottom of the onion intact.

2 Arrange the onions in a 8×8in (20×20cm) baking dish, well-side up, and fill the bottom of the dish with water. Cover the dish with foil and bake for 40 minutes, or until the onions are tender.

3 Meanwhile, in a medium saucepan, combine the stock, curry powder, and garam masala. Bring gradually to a boil and add the quinoa. Return to a boil then reduce to a simmer and cook, covered, for 15–18 minutes until tender. Remove from the heat and let sit, covered, for 5 minutes.

4 In a large mixing bowl, combine the cooked quinoa, black lentils, goat cheese, and ¼ cup (10g) cilantro. Thoroughly combine. Season with salt and pepper to taste.

5 Spoon an equal amount of quinoa mixture into each onion half. Bake, uncovered, for 20 minutes, or until the filling is toasted and warmed through. Garnish with the remaining 2 tablespoons of cilantro and serve immediately.

4 onions

1 cup (240ml) water

2¼ cups (550ml) vegetable stock

½ tsp curry powder

½ tsp garam masala

1 cup (175g) uncooked red, black, and white quinoa

¾ cup (140g) cooked black lentils

6oz (175g) crumbled goat cheese

¼ cup (10g) plus 2 tbsp chopped cilantro

salt and freshly ground black pepper

### Make it vegan

Replace the goat cheese with a nut cheese (see page 37).

### Make it with meat

Reduce the cooked black lentils to ½ cup (100g) and add ½ lb (225g) cooked ground lamb along with the lentils.

# Moth Bean Stuffed Sweet Potatoes

The surprising mix of sweet and savory in these baked potatoes makes for a truly luscious meal or hearty side dish.

**makes** 8   **prep** 15 min   **cook** 1 hr 15 min

1   Preheat the oven to 425°F (220°C) and line a baking sheet with foil.

2   Cut each sweet potato in half lengthwise. Lightly oil each cut side. Arrange the potatoes cut-side down on the baking sheet and bake for 30–40 minutes until tender all the way through.

3   To assemble, turn the sweet potato halves cut side up. With a fork, fluff the inside of the potatoes while keeping the skin intact. Top each potato half with an equal amount of moth beans (or lentils) and an equal amount of Brie. Season with salt and pepper.

4   Bake for an additional 8–10 minutes until the Brie is melted and gooey. Sprinkle each potato half with 2 tablespoons of pomegranate seeds and 2 tablespoons of cilantro. Serve immediately.

4 sweet potatoes, about 2lb (1kg) in total

2 cups (500g) cooked moth beans, or black lentils

8oz (225g) Brie cheese

salt and freshly ground black pepper

1 cup (175g) pomegranate seeds

1 cup (30g) coarsely chopped cilantro

## Make it with meat

Crumble 2oz (60g) cooked bacon into each sweet potato along with the pomegranate seeds.

# Baked Lentil Spaghetti Squash

For infusing your diet with complex carbohydrates, spaghetti squash is a healthy alternative to pasta. Each squash half is its own nutty, casserole-type dish in a self-contained serving.

**serves** 2   **prep** 25 min   **cook** 45 min

1 Preheat the oven to 375°F (190°C). Cut the spaghetti squash in half lengthwise and use a spoon to scrape the seeds out of each half. Drizzle each half with 1 tablespoon of oil, and arrange cut side down on a baking sheet. Cook for 30–35 minutes until tender but not mushy.

2 Meanwhile, in a medium mixing bowl, combine the lentils, walnuts, thyme, and lemon zest. Set aside until the squash is cooked.

3 With a fork, scrape the squash flesh to expose and fluff the spaghetti shreds. Season with salt and pepper. Divide the lentil filling evenly between the halves and crumble goat cheese over each. Bake for an additional 10 minutes, or until the cheese softens. Serve immediately, directly from the squash shell.

1 spaghetti squash (available from farmers' markets throughout winter and spring)

2 tbsp olive oil

1½ cups (450g) cooked green or Puy lentils

½ cup (60g) walnuts, toasted and coarsely chopped

1 tbsp thyme

zest of 1 lemon

salt and freshly ground black pepper

4oz (115g) soft goat cheese

### Make it vegan

Omit the goat cheese, or use a nut cheese (see page 37).

### Make it with meat

Reduce the lentils to 1 cup (225g) and add 4½oz (130g) cooked, seasoned ground turkey to the filling.

# Lima Bean Enchiladas

Tomatillos are a staple in Mexican sauces. Their tart, fruity flavor shines in this herby enchilada sauce, wonderfully set off by buttery beans and a sweet medley of vegetables.

**makes** 10  **prep** 55 min  **cook** 1 hr

1  Preheat the oven to 350°F (180°C). On a lightly oiled baking sheet, arrange the tomatillos, jalapeños, and onion. Roast for 20–25 minutes until tender. Leave to cool slightly. To make the sauce, transfer the roasted vegetables to a blender and combine with the cilantro sprigs and stock. Blend until completely smooth. Season with salt and pepper.

2  To make the filling, in a large frying pan heat the oil over medium-low heat. Add the garlic and cook for 1–2 minutes until soft. Add the zucchini and corn and cook, covered, for an additional 2–3 minutes until the zucchini starts to become tender. Stir in the spinach, cumin, coriander, and red pepper flakes. Cover and cook for another 3–4 minutes until the spinach wilts slightly. Stir in the lima beans. Season with salt and pepper to taste. Remove from the heat and leave to cool slightly.

3  Lightly oil a 9×12in (23×30cm) glass or ceramic baking dish. Lightly coat the bottom with sauce. To assemble, work with one tortilla at a time on a clean, flat work surface. Place 4 tablespoons of filling onto the tortilla and top with 1½–2 tablespoons of grated cheese. Roll tightly and place seam-side down in the dish. Repeat to make 10 enchiladas in total.

4  Top the enchiladas with the remaining sauce. Sprinkle the remaining cheese over the top. Cover with foil and bake for 15 minutes. Uncover and bake for another 10 minutes, or until the cheese melts. Garnish with chopped cilantro and serve immediately.

1½lb (675g) tomatillos, husks removed, coarsely chopped (or small, unripe tomatoes, coarsely chopped)

2 medium jalapeños, seeded and chopped

1 onion, chopped

1 cup (30g) cilantro sprigs

⅔ cup (175ml) vegetable stock

salt and freshly ground black pepper

1 tbsp vegetable oil

1 clove garlic, finely chopped

2 zucchinis, diced

1 cup (150g) fresh corn kernels

4 cups (175g) baby spinach

1½ tsp ground cumin

1 tsp ground coriander

pinch red pepper flakes

1½ cups (225g) cooked lima beans

10 small corn tortillas

8oz (225g) mozzarella cheese, grated

½ cup (15g) chopped cilantro

### Why not try ...
Use crumbled feta instead of grated mozzarella. Place 1 tablespoon inside each enchilada and sprinkle the rest on top.

### Make it vegan

Use a nut cheese instead of mozzarella (see page 37).

### Make it with meat

Omit one zucchini and add 4½oz (125g) cooked, shredded chicken or pork to the filling.

# Pigeon Pea Samosa Bake

Filled with the unique aromas and flavors of Indian spiced potatoes and pigeon peas, this casserole with its crunchy phyllo topping is a nod to traditional samosa pastry.

**serves** 8   **prep** 30 min   **cook** 45 min

**1** Preheat the oven to 350°F (180°C). Lightly oil a 9in (23cm) round baking dish.

**2** Bring a large saucepan of water to a rapid boil. Add the potatoes and cook for 8–10 minutes until tender to the point of a knife. Meanwhile, place the green peas in a sieve or colander. When the potatoes are cooked, pour the potatoes and hot water over the peas. Let drain thoroughly.

**3** In a large frying pan, heat 2 tablespoons of ghee over medium-low heat until shimmering. Add the onion and chile and cook for 2–3 minutes until soft. Incorporate the ginger, coriander, garam masala, cumin, turmeric, cayenne, curry powder, and water. Cook for an additional minute until the spices are warmed through.

**4** Add the potatoes and green peas, pigeon peas (or black-eyed peas), stock, cilantro, and remaining 1 tablespoon ghee. Stir to combine. Season with salt and pepper to taste. Remove from the heat.

**5** Transfer the mixture to the baking dish. Crinkle the phyllo sheets and place atop the potato mixture. Bake for 20–25 minutes until the phyllo pastry is golden brown, then serve.

4 cups (550g) peeled and diced potatoes

1 cup (115g) frozen green peas, thawed

3 tbsp ghee

1 small onion, diced

1 small green chile, seeded and finely chopped

¼ tsp ground ginger

¼ tsp ground coriander

¾ tsp garam masala

1 tsp ground cumin

¼ tsp ground turmeric

¼ tsp ground cayenne pepper

¾ tsp curry powder

1 tbsp water

½ cup (75g) cooked pigeon peas or black-eyed peas

⅓ cup (90ml) vegetable stock

⅓ cup (10g) chopped cilantro

salt and freshly ground black pepper

4 sheets of frozen phyllo pastry, thawed

**Why not try ...**

For an aromatic garnish, sprinkle the pastry with crushed cumin seeds before baking.

**Make it vegan**

Replace the ghee with canola oil.

**Make it with meat**

Add 4½oz (125g) cooked, seasoned ground lamb with the peas in step 4

# Ratatouille Casserole with Farro and Feta

A mix of baked Mediterranean vegetables, tomato sauce, and tender farro is topped with contrasting salty feta cheese for a warm and filling meal that is perfect at any time of the year.

**serves** 4   **prep** 10 min, plus overnight soaking   **cook** 1 hr 30 min

1  Place the farro in a large bowl, cover with water, and leave to soak overnight or for up to 8 hours. Then drain any remaining water, rinse under running water, and drain well again. Set aside.

2  Preheat the oven to 350°F (180°C). Place the eggplant cubes in a colander, sprinkle with the salt, and press down with a heavy object. Leave to draw out the water and any bitterness.

3  Place the peppers, zucchini, onions, and eggplant in a 2 quart (2 liter) casserole dish. Spread them out evenly and drizzle with the oil. Add the farro to the dish and toss lightly to mix with the vegetables.

4  Place the tomatoes, stock, rosemary, and garlic in a large bowl and mix to combine. Add the mixture to the casserole and mix well. Cover, place in the oven, and bake for 1 hour and 15 minutes or until the vegetables are tender and the farro is cooked.

5  Remove from the heat, take off the lid, and sprinkle in the feta. Return to the oven, uncovered, and cook for about 15 minutes or until the feta starts to turn golden. Remove from the heat and season to taste if needed. Garnish with basil and serve hot.

½ cup (100g) uncooked farro

1 eggplant, cut into cubes

½ tsp salt

2 red or orange peppers, seeded and cut into bite-size pieces

1 zucchini, cut into bite-size pieces

1 red onion, finely chopped

1 tbsp light olive oil

14oz (400g) can diced tomatoes

1 cup (250ml) vegetable stock

¼ tsp dried rosemary

1 clove garlic, finely chopped

7oz (200g) feta cheese, crumbled

salt and freshly ground black pepper

2 tsp chopped basil, to serve

## Make it vegan

Omit the feta cheese or replace it with a nut cheese (see page 37).

# Pasta and Grains

Pasta and grain dishes are simple to prepare and make the perfect flexitarian meal—you can easily substitute ingredients to meet your dietary requirements.

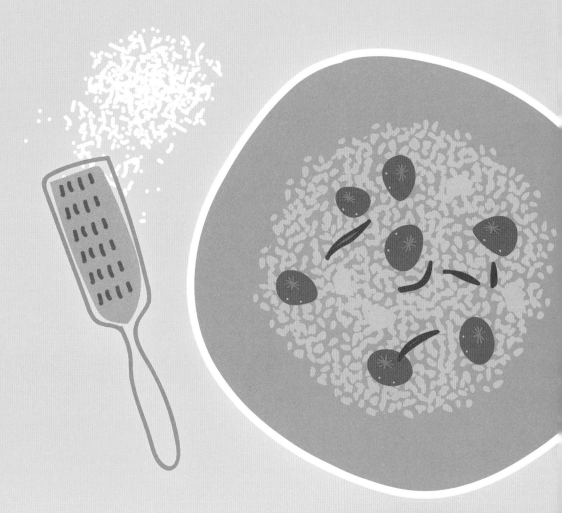

# Shaved Asparagus, Mint, and Edamame Spaghetti

This vibrant green sauce is perfect for a light meal. Mint provides an unexpected and refreshing flavor that is delicious served with the tender asparagus and edamame.

**serves** 4   **prep** 10 min   **cook** 20 min

1 Bring a large pan of salted water to a boil. To prepare the asparagus, place each spear flat on a cutting board and use a peeler to shave into very thin slices.

2 Cook the edamame in the boiling water for 1 minute. Remove with a slotted spoon and put into a bowl of ice water.

3 Add the spaghetti to the boiling water and cook according to the package instructions until just al dente. When the spaghetti is cooked, drain and reserve ½ cup (120ml) cooking water. Set the spaghetti aside.

4 Meanwhile, when the spaghetti is nearly cooked, heat the olive oil in a large, nonstick frying pan. Add the asparagus and leek and cook for 2 minutes, stirring frequently, until the asparagus starts to soften. Add the garlic and edamame and cook for 1 minute more. Remove from the heat.

5 Add the ricotta and 4 tablespoons of the reserved cooking water to the pasta pan. Whisk until smooth, adding more cooking water as necessary. Add the asparagus mixture to the pan and mix together over a low heat.

6 Return the spaghetti to the pan, and add the mint and Parmesan. Toss well. Season well with salt and pepper. Divide among 4 serving plates and serve immediately with more Parmesan, mint leaves, and a drizzle of olive oil on top.

salt and freshly ground black pepper

8oz (225g) large asparagus, trimmed

¾ cup (115g) frozen shelled edamame

14oz (400g) dried whole wheat spaghetti

2 tbsp olive oil, plus extra to serve

1 large leek, white parts only, trimmed and julienned

1 large clove garlic, crushed

4oz (115g) ricotta cheese

1 large handful fresh mint, finely chopped, plus extra whole leaves to garnish

2 tbsp grated Parmesan cheese, plus extra to serve

### Make it vegan

Instead of the ricotta, put 4oz (115g) firm tofu, 2 tbsp lemon juice, 1 tbsp nutritional yeast, and 1 tbsp extra virgin olive oil in a blender and pulse until it is semi-pureed. Use this tofu mixture in place of the ricotta in step 5. Omit the Parmesan cheese or use a vegan alternative.

# Roasted Cauliflower and Mint Orecchiette

The hearty yet delicately shaped pasta is a perfect partner for creamy roasted cauliflower and light, fresh herbs. If you can't find yellow cauliflower, substitute with white cauliflower.

**serves** 4   **prep** 5 min   **cook** 20 min

1   Preheat the oven to 400°F (200°C). Bring a large pan of salted water to a boil. To prepare the cauliflower: in a large bowl, mix the olive oil, garlic, and red pepper flakes. Season with salt and pepper to taste. Add the cauliflower and toss with your hands, making sure the seasoning is rubbed in well.

2   Evenly spread the cauliflower in a large, metal roasting pan. Transfer to the top rack of the oven and roast for 15 minutes, or until just cooked and browned in places.

3   Meanwhile, cook the orecchiette in the boiling water according to the package instructions until just al dente. Drain and reserve 1 cup (240ml) cooking water.

4   In a large, cast-iron frying pan, melt the butter and olive oil over medium heat. Add about 2 tablespoons cooking water and allow to bubble. Add the orecchiette and cook for 1 to 2 minutes until the pasta has absorbed most of the liquid.

5   Gently toss the cauliflower in the pasta. (Be sure to include all the crispy bits of garlic and red pepper flakes from the roasting pan.) Transfer to 4 serving dishes and top with equal amounts of the parsley and mint. Serve immediately with Parmesan.

salt and freshly ground black pepper

4¼ cups (400g) dried orecchiette

2 tbsp unsalted butter

2 tbsp olive oil

2 tbsp finely chopped flat-leaf parsley

2 tbsp mint

grated Parmesan cheese, to serve

**For the cauliflower**

4 tbsp olive oil

2 cloves garlic, crushed

1 tsp red pepper flakes

1lb (450g) yellow (or white) cauliflower, cut into florets

## Make it vegan

Replace the butter with a vegetable oil spread and the cheese with a plant-based Parmesan.

# Sweet Potato Gnocchi and Hazelnut Gremolata

The zesty flavor and crunchy texture of the hazelnut gremolata contrasts well with the soft, slightly sweet gnocchi. Creamy, rich cheese sauce makes this dish truly decadent.

**serves** 4–6  **prep** 40 min  **cook** 1 hr 20 min, plus cooling

1 Preheat the oven to 450°F (230°C). To make the gnocchi dough: wash and dry the sweet potatoes. Cut a small slit in the skins. Place in the oven and bake for 45 minutes, or until fork-tender. Remove from the oven and leave to cool completely.

2 Cut the cooled potatoes in half. Scoop the flesh into a medium bowl and mash with a potato masher. Stir in the sage and Parmesan, and season with salt and pepper. Stir in the sweet rice flour, millet flour, and almond flour, mixing together well to form a soft, sticky dough.

3 To shape the gnocchi: place the dough onto a work surface lightly dusted with flour. Cut the dough into 4 sections and work with 1 section at a time, keeping the rest covered with plastic wrap. With your hands, roll a section of dough into a long, thin cylinder, about 1in (2.5cm) wide. Cut the cylinder into disks about ³⁄₄in (2cm) thick. Roll each disk into a small ball in your hands, then place on the work surface and tap to flatten slightly. When all are shaped, run the tines of a fork over the tops of the gnocchi to make indentations.

4 To make the gremolata: in a nonstick frying pan, toast the hazelnuts over medium heat for 2 minutes, stirring frequently, until golden brown in places. Remove from the heat. Once cool, rub them well in a clean kitchen towel to remove as much of the skins as possible. Set aside to cool, then finely chop.

5 Bring a large pan of salted water to a boil. In a small bowl, mix together the hazelnuts, parsley, lemon zest, and Parmesan. Season well with black pepper.

6 Reduce the boiling water to a simmer. Working in batches, add the gnocchi to the water and cook for 4 to 5 minutes until they float to the surface. Remove with a slotted spoon and place on a plate lined with paper towel to absorb the water. Continue until all are cooked.

7 To make the cheese sauce: add the cream and grated cheese to a small saucepan. Scatter the sweet rice flour over the surface and whisk in. Slowly bring to a boil, stirring constantly, until the sauce thickens and starts to bubble. Reduce the heat to low and cook for 1 minute more until thick and smooth. Season with black pepper.

8 Grease a large, shallow, ovenproof dish. Arrange the gnocchi in an even layer in the dish. Spread the cheese sauce over the top. Transfer to the top rack of the oven and bake, uncovered, for 10 to 12 minutes until the top is golden brown and crispy. Remove from the oven and leave to cool for 5 to 10 minutes. Scatter the top with the hazelnut gremolata before serving.

## For the gnocchi dough

2 medium sweet potatoes, about 10oz (300g) in total

1 tsp very finely chopped sage

⅓ cup (30g) finely grated Parmesan cheese

salt and freshly ground black pepper

⅓ cup (60g) sweet rice flour

⅓ cup (60g) millet flour

⅓ cup (60g) almond flour

## For the gremolata

⅛ cup (15g) coarsely chopped hazelnuts

1 tbsp finely chopped flat-leaf parsley

½ tsp lemon zest

1 tbsp freshly grated Parmesan cheese

## For the cheese sauce

½ cup (120ml) heavy cream

1 cup (115g) grated cheese, such as Gruyère or fontina

1 tsp sweet rice flour

# Citrus Zucchini Cannelloni with Goat Cheese

Grilling the zucchini slices helps them become soft and easy to roll. The lightly charred flavor is a nice addition to the cheesy and lemony filling. Serve with a crisp green salad.

**serves** 4 **prep** 15 min **cook** 40 min, plus cooling

1 Heat a cast-iron grill pan and lightly brush with olive oil. Grill the zucchini slices for 1 to 2 minutes on each side until soft and lightly marked with grill marks. At the same time, in a nonstick frying pan, toast the pine nuts over medium heat for 2 to 3 minutes, turning frequently, until golden brown. Set aside to cool. Blot any excess moisture with paper towel once cool.

2 In a small bowl, beat together the goat cheese, basil, lemon zest, and pine nuts. Season well with salt and pepper.

3 To assemble the cannelloni: portion a large, walnut-sized spoonful of goat cheese mixture and place on a zucchini slice. Spread out the cheese along the length of the slice. Roll the slice up. Place in a lightly oiled, shallow ovenproof dish. Repeat to assemble the remaining cannelloni.

4 Preheat the oven to 450°F (230°C). To make the cheese sauce: in a small saucepan, melt the butter over medium heat. Remove from the heat and whisk in the rice flour. Continue to whisk, slowly adding in the milk. Return to the heat and slowly bring to a boil, whisking frequently, until the mixture thickens. Reduce the heat to low and continue to cook for 2 to 3 minutes. Season well with salt and pepper and add most of the grated cheese, reserving some to sprinkle over the top. Whisk the sauce until the cheese melts, adding more milk if needed to help achieve a pourable consistency. Remove from the heat.

5 Pour the sauce over the cannelloni and top with the remaining grated cheese. Transfer to the top rack of the oven. Cook, uncovered, for 15 to 20 minutes until the top is golden brown and the cannelloni are cooked through. Remove from the oven and leave to cool for 10 minutes, or until the cheese settles. Garnish with the basil and a drizzle of olive oil, and serve.

olive oil, for greasing and to serve

2 fat zucchini, about 10oz (300g) each, trimmed and cut into 12 thin slices lengthwise with a mandoline

½ cup (60g) pine nuts

7oz (200g) soft goat cheese, room temperature

2 tbsp finely chopped basil, plus whole leaves to garnish

zest of 1 small or ½ large lemon

salt and freshly ground black pepper

### For the cheese sauce

1 tbsp (15g) unsalted butter

1½ tbsp (15g) sweet rice flour

½ cup (100ml) whole milk

1oz (30g) strong cheese, such as Cheddar, grated

---

**Make it vegan**

Use a nut cheese (see page 37) in place of the goat cheese. And replace the cheese sauce with vegan Béchamel Sauce (see page 42), adding in 1oz (30g) plant-based cheese if you'd like.

# Rainbow Lentil Meatballs with Arrabbiata Sauce

Lentil meatballs and spicy tomato sauce are a vegetarian alternative to the comfort food classic, loaded with protein and fiber. Serve with pasta or bread and Parmesan cheese.

**serves** 18   **prep** 15 min   **cook** 40 min

1   Preheat the oven to 350°F (180°C). Lightly oil a baking sheet. In a large mixing bowl, combine the red and brown lentils, egg, breadcrumbs, garlic powder, oregano, lemon zest, and cayenne.

2   With your hands, form approximately 1 tablespoon of the lentil mixture into a meatball and place on the baking tray. Repeat with the remaining mixture. Bake for 25 minutes, rotating the meatballs halfway through.

3   Meanwhile, to make the arrabbiata sauce, in a saucepan warm the oil over medium-low heat. Add the onion and cook for 2 minutes, or until soft. Add the tomatoes and red pepper flakes. Simmer over low heat for 15 minutes, or until the sauce is warmed through. Season with salt and pepper to taste.

4   Serve the meatballs with cooked spaghetti, topped with the sauce.

1½ cups (300g) cooked red lentils, thoroughly drained

½ cup (85g) cooked brown lentils, thoroughly drained

1 large egg, lightly beaten

¾ cup (45g) panko breadcrumbs

½ tsp garlic powder

1 tsp dried oregano

zest of 1 large lemon

¼ tsp ground cayenne pepper

2 tbsp olive oil

1 small onion, finely chopped

2 (14oz/400g) cans diced tomatoes

1 tbsp red pepper flakes

salt and freshly ground black pepper

### Make it vegan

Replace the egg with 3 tbsp aquafaba.

### Make it with meat

Add 8oz (225g) ground beef or crumbled Italian sausage along with the onion in step 3.

# Three Bean Paella

This colorful twist on the classic Spanish dish features a trio of meaty pulses in addition to saffron-scented rice, roasted red peppers, and tangy green olives.

**serves** 10   **prep** 35 min   **cook** 1 hr 5 min

1  In a 10in (25cm) paella pan or large cast-iron frying pan, warm the oil over medium heat until shimmering. Add the onion and cook for 2 minutes, or until it starts to soften. Stir in the garlic and cook for 30 seconds, or until fragrant. Incorporate the saffron, red pepper flakes, tomatoes, and paprika. Stir in the rice and cook for 2–3 minutes.

2  Add the stock to the rice mixture and stir. Bring to a boil then reduce the heat to low and cook, covered, for 20 minutes. Stir in the navy beans, pigeon peas (or black-eyed peas), and kidney beans. Cover again and cook for an additional 10 minutes. Scatter the peas across the top and cook without stirring, covered, for another 10 minutes, or until the beans and peas are warmed through. Remove from the heat.

3  Season with salt and pepper to taste. Arrange the red pepper strips and olives evenly across the top. Cover and let the paella stand for 5 minutes. Garnish with lemon wedges and parsley, then serve.

2 tbsp olive oil

1 onion, chopped

3 cloves garlic, finely chopped

pinch saffron threads

pinch red pepper flakes

1¼ cups (225g) chopped tomatoes

1 tsp smoked paprika

1lb (450g) uncooked paella rice, such as Bomba or Calasparra

2½ cups (750ml) vegetable stock

1 cup (175g) cooked navy beans

⅔ cup (115g) cooked pigeon peas or black-eyed peas

¾ cup (125g) cooked kidney beans

½ cup (60g) frozen peas, thawed

salt and freshly ground black pepper

⅔ cup (60g) roasted red pepper, drained and cut in strips

2oz (60g) pitted green Spanish olives, sliced

1 large lemon, cut into 8 wedges

flat-leaf parsley, to garnish

### Make it with fish

Add 8oz (225g) cooked, peeled shrimp along with the red pepper strips in step 3.

# Egyptian Rice

This is a fragrant mix of pantry staples—rice and lentils. Dukkah is an Egyptian mix of spices, roasted nuts, and ground sesame seeds. Add toasted almonds or hazelnuts, if you wish.

**serves** 4   **prep** 15 min   **cook** 1 hr 15 min

1 Put the lentils and bay leaf in a heavy-bottomed pan and pour over the stock. Season with salt and pepper, then bring to a boil, reduce the heat to a simmer, cover with the lid, and cook for about 20 minutes (depending on the lentil package instructions). Remove the lid and cook for a further 10 minutes or so until the lentils are beginning to soften. Turn off the heat, put the lid back on, and set aside.

2 Put the rice in a separate pan, cover with water so it just covers the top of the rice, and bring to a boil. Reduce to a simmer and cook gently, partially covered with the lid, for about 10 minutes or until the rice is cooked through—you may need to top up the hot water if the rice is becoming dry. Turn off the heat, cover with the lid, and set aside—the rice will continue to steam.

3 Heat the oil in a large fire-resistant casserole dish over medium heat, add the onions, and cook for 8–10 minutes until they just begin to crisp slightly. Season with salt and pepper, stir in the garlic, cumin, and dukkah spice (if using), and cook for 1 minute. Drain the lentils, then add lentils and rice to the onion mixture, stirring well so all the grains and lentils are coated and everything is heated through. Add the lemon juice and most of the herbs, remembering to remove the bay leaf. Serve topped with the feta or spoon over a tomato-based sauce or plain yogurt. Sprinkle over the remaining fresh herbs to garnish.

1 cup (200g) Puy lentils, rinsed and picked over for any stones

1 bay leaf

3 cups (900ml) hot vegetable stock

salt and freshly ground black pepper

1 cup (200g) easy-cook basmati rice

2 tbsp olive oil

2 large onions, sliced

3 cloves garlic, grated

1 tsp cumin

3 tsp Dukkah spice (optional)

juice of 1 lemon

small handful flat-leaf parsley, finely chopped

small handful mint, finely chopped

small handful cilantro, finely chopped

1⅓ cups (200g) crumbled feta cheese

## Make it vegan

Replace the feta cheese with nut cheese (see page 37).

# Vegetable Biryani

In this dish, the rice is cooked first and then is gently steamed in the spiced vegetable mixture. Adjust the vegetable list to suit your refrigerator, adding more or fewer varieties as you wish.

**serves** 6  **prep** 30 min  **cook** 1 hr 15 min

1 Preheat the oven to 350°F (180°C). In a pan of simmering water, cook the rice for 10 minutes or until just tender. Drain and set aside. Cook the carrot and potatoes in a pan of boiling water for about 5 minutes until almost tender. Then add the cauliflower and cook for a further 6-8 minutes until all the vegetables are tender. Drain and set aside.

2 Heat the oil in a large heavy-bottomed pan over medium heat, add the onion, and cook for 4-5 minutes until soft. Add the red and green peppers and the zucchini, and cook for 5 minutes, stirring occasionally. Add the boiled vegetables and frozen peas, then stir in the turmeric, chili powder, coriander, curry paste, and cumin seeds. Cook for a further 5 minutes, then stir in the stock.

3 Spoon half the rice into an ovenproof dish and top with the vegetable mixture. Top with the remaining rice, cover with foil, and bake for about 30 minutes until hot. Scatter over the cashews and serve with naan, mango chutney, lime pickle, or raita.

1½ cups (350g) basmati rice

1 large carrot, peeled and sliced

2 potatoes, peeled and chopped into small pieces

½ cauliflower, cut into small florets

3 tbsp vegetable oil

1 red onion, chopped

1 red pepper, seeded and chopped

1 green pepper, seeded and chopped

1 zucchini, chopped

½ cup (85g) frozen peas

1 tsp ground turmeric

1 tsp mild chili powder

2 tsp ground coriander

2 tsp mild curry paste

1 tsp cumin seeds

¾ cup (150ml) hot vegetable stock

2oz (60g) cashews, lightly toasted

### Make it with meat

Add 1lb 2oz (500g) cubed chicken thigh fillets to the pan after the onions in step 2. Stir over the heat for 5 minutes and then continue as per the recipe.

# Roasted Vegetable Farro Risotto

This rich and delicious risotto uses farro for its chewy texture and slightly sweet flavor. The addition of roasted vegetables makes this a warm and satisfying meal.

**serves** 4   **prep** 15 min   **cook** 40 min

1   Preheat the oven to 400°F (200°C). Heat 1 tablespoon of the oil in a large saucepan over medium heat. Add the onion and cook for about 5 minutes, stirring frequently, until softened. Then add the farro, stir to mix, and cook gently for 1–2 minutes.

2   Stir the wine into the pan and leave to cook until all the liquid has been absorbed. Then add the stock a ladleful at a time, stirring constantly, allowing the liquid to be fully absorbed before adding more. Once all the liquid has been absorbed, add the Parmesan and thyme, and season to taste. Remove from the heat.

3   Meanwhile, arrange the red peppers, zucchini, and tomatoes on a baking sheet. Drizzle over the remaining oil and season with salt and pepper. Transfer to the oven and roast the vegetables for 20–25 minutes, stirring occasionally, until cooked through and golden. Stir the roasted vegetables into the risotto and serve immediately.

3 tbsp light olive oil

1 small onion, finely chopped

¾ cup (150g) uncooked farro

½ cup (120ml) white wine

4 cups (1 liter) hot vegetable stock

½ cup (50g) freshly grated Parmesan cheese

1 tbsp finely chopped thyme

sea salt and freshly ground black pepper

1 red pepper, seeded and thinly sliced

1 zucchini, diced

5½oz (150g) cherry tomatoes

### Make it with fish

Stir in 1lb 2oz (500g) cooked, peeled shrimp to the risotto with the roasted vegetables in step 3.

# Red Peppers Stuffed with Artichoke Barley Risotto

These lightly roasted sweet red peppers are the perfect vessels for a creamy barley risotto dotted with artichoke hearts and are a delightful change from the conventional stuffed peppers.

**serves** 6  **prep** 10 min  **cook** 35 min

1 Heat 2 tablespoons of the oil in a large saucepan over medium heat. Add the onion and cook, stirring frequently, for 5–10 minutes or until translucent and lightly browned. Then add the barley, stir to mix, and cook for a further 1–2 minutes.

2 Stir the wine into the pan and leave to cook until all the liquid has been absorbed. Then add the stock a ladleful at a time, stirring constantly, allowing the liquid to be fully absorbed before adding more. Once all the stock has been added, cook, stirring constantly, for a further 2–3 minutes or until all the liquid has been absorbed. Remove from the heat, stir in the Parmesan and artichoke hearts, and season to taste.

3 Preheat the oven to 350°F (180°C). Slice the red peppers in half lengthwise. Then, core, seed, and remove the white ribs from the inside and discard. Rub the peppers with the remaining oil and place on a baking sheet lined with foil. Roast in the oven for 15 minutes, until softened. Remove from the heat. Divide the risotto mixture into 6 equal parts and use to fill the peppers. Serve immediately.

4 tbsp extra virgin olive oil

1 small onion, diced

1 cup (225g) uncooked barley

½ cup (125ml) white wine

4 cups (1 liter) warm vegetable stock

1 cup (100g) freshly grated Parmesan cheese

12oz (350g) artichoke hearts, chopped

salt and freshly ground black pepper

6 red peppers

### Make it vegan

Simply omit the Parmesan cheese or replace it with a plant-based Parmesan or nut cheese (see page 37).

# Cauliflower Hazelnut Polenta

It may seem fussy to skin the hazelnuts, but the skins can be quite bitter and will change the taste of the dish if left on. The sweetness of the roasted nuts contrasts well with the cauliflower and the ripeness of the Manchego.

**serves** 4   **prep** 15 min   **cook** 55 min

1   Preheat the oven to 350°F (180°C). Spread the hazelnuts out on a baking sheet, place in the oven, and toast for 10-15 minutes or until they are well browned with the skins peeling off. Leave them to cool slightly. Then place them between two pieces of paper towel and rub to remove the skins. Coarsely chop the hazelnuts and set aside.

2   Increase the heat to 400°F (200°C). Place the cauliflower on a large baking sheet, drizzle over the oil, and season well. Place in the oven and roast for 30 minutes, stirring occasionally, until golden brown and cooked through. Remove from the heat, drizzle over the lemon juice, and set aside.

3   For the polenta, place the milk and water in a large, lidded saucepan. Add ¼ teaspoon salt and a good grinding of pepper. Bring to a boil, then reduce the heat to medium-low. Gradually add one-third of the polenta, stirring constantly, until well combined. Then add the remaining polenta, stirring constantly, and cook for about 10 minutes or until it is well combined and smooth.

4   Reduce the heat to low and cover partially. Cook for a further 15 minutes, stirring occasionally to ensure it does not stick to the bottom, until it is creamy. Add a little more water or milk to the pan if the polenta seems too thick. Then stir in the butter and cheese and mix well to incorporate. Remove from the heat. Spoon the polenta into serving bowls and top with the hazelnuts and cauliflower. Garnish with the parsley and serve immediately.

½ cup (75g) hazelnuts

1lb (450g) cauliflower, cut into florets

1 tbsp olive oil

salt and freshly ground black pepper

juice of half a lemon

**For the polenta**

2 cups (500ml) milk, plus extra if needed

2 cups (500ml) water

1 cup (150g) coarse polenta

3 tbsp unsalted butter

⅓ cup (30g) grated Manchego cheese, plus extra to serve

handful flat-leaf parsley, coarsely chopped, to garnish

**Why not try ...**

Instead of Manchego cheese, try using Pecorino Romano. Parmesan will work, too, however it has a stronger flavor and saltiness so you might not need as much.

**Make it vegan**

To make the polenta, bring 4 cups (1 liter) vegetable stock to a boil in a large, lidded saucepan. Add the polenta and cook according to steps 3 and 4. When the polenta is smooth and thick stir in ¼ cup (60ml) soy milk, 3 tbsp nutritional yeast, and 1–2 tbsp plant-based spread.

# Desserts

Desserts and sweet treats can still be enjoyed on a flexitarian diet. These recipes include plenty of vegan variations, too, making them perfect for when you are reducing your intake of animal products.

# Strawberry Polenta Shortcakes

These little "sandwiches" are a lovely adaptation of the traditional shortcake. They make excellent use of polenta to produce the perfect dessert for summer, when you can take advantage of a glut of strawberries.

**serves** 6 **prep** 30 min **cook** 40 min

1  Preheat the oven to 375°F (190°C). Line two baking sheets with parchment paper and set aside. In a large saucepan, bring the water to a simmer. Then add the polenta and cook for 2–3 minutes, stirring constantly, until it has thickened. Remove from the heat and leave to cool for about 2 minutes.

2  Add the oil, sugar, and vanilla extract and mix well. Divide the mixture equally between the two baking sheets, spreading it out to a ¼in- (5mm-) thick layer. Place in the oven and bake for 30 minutes or until the polenta is spongy and slightly firm to the touch. It should easily pull away from the paper. Remove from the heat and leave to cool.

3  Place the cooled polenta on a clean work surface and use a cookie cutter to cut out twelve 3in- (8cm-) wide rounds. Place the heavy cream in a large bowl and whisk until it is thick and holds its shape. Place one-third of the strawberries in a bowl and crush with the back of a fork. Add half the confectioners sugar and mix well to combine. Cut the remaining strawberries into thin slices.

4  To assemble the shortcakes, lay one polenta round on each of six plates. Top them with 1 tablespoon of the whipped cream, 1 tablespoon of the strawberry and sugar mixture, and a few slices of strawberries. Place the remaining polenta rounds on top and gently pat them dry with paper towel. Dust with confectioners sugar and serve immediately.

4 cups (1 liter) water

1¼ cups (200g) polenta

2 tbsp light olive oil

3 tbsp (40g) sugar

1 tsp vanilla extract

1¼ cups (300ml) heavy cream

1lb 2oz (500g) strawberries

3 tbsp (20g) confectioners sugar

### Make it vegan

Refrigerate a 14oz (400ml) can coconut milk overnight. Scoop the thick, solid milk at the top of the can into a bowl. Using an electric mixer, beat the coconut milk on medium-high until smooth. Add 2 tbsp confectioners sugar and continue beating until the milk is fluffy and resembles whipped cream. Use this in place of the whipped cream in step 4.

# Sweet Spiced Freekeh with Fresh Figs

Inspired by the cuisine of the Middle East, in this dish the freekeh is cooked with sweet spices to enhance its flavor and served with honey, pistachios, and figs for an aromatic and mouth-watering dessert.

**serves** 4   **prep** 5 min   **cook** 25 min

1. Place the freekeh, star anise, cardamom, cinnamon, ginger, and nutmeg in a large saucepan. Add the salt and cover with the water. Place the pan over medium heat and bring to a boil. Then reduce the heat to a simmer and cook for about 15 minutes or until all the liquid has been absorbed.

2. Meanwhile, preheat the broiler to medium. Grease and line a baking sheet with parchment paper. Cut a cross in the top of each fig, cutting almost to the bottom so they open up like a flower. Place on the baking sheet and drizzle with 2 tablespoons of honey. Place under the broiler and cook for 10 minutes or until the figs are lightly broiled.

3. Remove and discard the star anise and cardamom pods. Add the remaining honey to the cooked freekeh and mix well. Divide the freekeh mixture between four plates. Top each plate with two figs and a quarter of the pistachios. Garnish with mint and drizzle with honey, if you wish. Serve with Greek yogurt.

½ cup (100g) cracked freekeh

1 star anise

4 cardamom pods

1 tsp ground cinnamon

½ tsp grated fresh ginger

¼ tsp ground nutmeg

¼ tsp salt

2 cups (500ml) water

8 fresh figs, stems removed

4 tbsp honey, plus extra to serve

⅓ cup (40g) coarsely chopped pistachios

2 tbsp chopped mint

4 tbsp Greek yogurt, to serve

## Why not try ...

In place of the freekeh, you can use the same quantity of polenta.

## Make it vegan

Replace the honey with agave nectar and the Greek yogurt with coconut yogurt (see page 38).

# Almond Polenta Cake with Raspberries

This gluten-free cake is perfect for satisfying your sweet tooth while staying away from flour. The polenta and almonds give the cake a crumbly texture that beautifully offsets the tartness of the raspberries.

**serves** 8-10   **prep** 15 min, plus cooling   **cook** 45 min

1 Preheat the oven to 350°F (180°C). Grease and line a 9in (23cm) springform pan with parchment paper. Cream the butter and sugar with an electric hand mixer for 2 minutes or until light and fluffy. Add the eggs one at a time, mixing well between additions. Then add the almond extract and mix for 2 minutes until fully incorporated.

2 Place the ground almonds, polenta, and baking powder in a separate bowl and mix well. Lightly fold the dry mixture into the butter, sugar, and egg mixture until just smooth. Gently fold the raspberries into the batter. Spoon the batter into the prepared tin, smooth over the surface, and scatter over the slivered almonds.

3 Bake the cake for 45 minutes or until golden brown and a skewer inserted into the center comes out with only a few crumbs. Leave the cake in the pan to cool slightly. Then transfer to a wire rack to cool completely before serving. Store in the fridge, in an airtight container, for up to 3 days.

¾ cup (200g) unsalted butter

1¼ cups (230g) superfine sugar

3 large eggs

1 tsp almond extract

2 cups (200g) ground almonds

⅔ cup (100g) polenta

1½ tsp baking powder

1½ cups (200g) raspberries

¼ cup (20g) slivered almonds

### Make it vegan

Instead of unsalted butter, use the same amount of vegetable oil spread. Whisk together 3 tbsp flax seeds with 9 tbsp warm water and let it stand for 15 minutes. Use this mixture in place of the eggs in step 1.

# Chocolate Chip, Peanut, and Buckwheat Cookies

Gluten-free buckwheat flour adds to the nuttiness of these delicious cookies. Perfect for children and adults alike, enjoy them with a cup of tea or your morning coffee.

**makes** 12 large cookies   **prep** 30 min, plus chilling and cooling   **cook** 15 min

1 In a large bowl, cream together the butter and sugar with an electric hand mixer until light and fluffy. Then beat the egg into the mixture until well combined.

2 Place the flour, salt, and baking powder in a separate bowl and mix well. Fold the dry mixture into the butter, sugar, and egg mixture, a little at a time, until thoroughly incorporated. Add the chocolate chips and peanuts to the mixture and stir well to incorporate. Cover the dough with plastic wrap and chill in the fridge for about 30 minutes. Preheat the oven to 350°F (180°C). Line two baking sheets with parchment paper.

3 Place golf ball-sized portions of dough on the prepared baking sheets and flatten them gently. Make sure they are placed at least 2in (5cm) apart, as they will spread while baking. Bake the cookies for about 15 minutes, until they start to turn golden but still look a little underbaked. Remove from the heat and leave on the baking sheet for at least 10 minutes to cool and firm up. Then transfer to a wire rack to cool completely. Store in an airtight container.

½ cup (110g) unsalted butter

¾ cup (175g) brown sugar, packed

1 large egg

1⅔ cups (200g) buckwheat flour

¼ tsp salt

½ tsp baking powder

½ cup (85g) dark chocolate chips

½ cup (85g) salted peanuts

### Make it vegan

Replace the unsalted butter with the same amount of vegetable oil spread. Mix 1 tbsp flax seeds with 3 tbsp warm water and let it sit for 15 minutes. Add this mixture instead of the egg in step 1. Most dark chocolate is vegan, but check the label to be sure.

# Apple and Cinnamon Crumble

This is a beloved dessert, and deservedly so. A good crumble topping should be loosely patted down over the filling, and made with irregular-sized lumps of butter that melt and create a fudgelike texture during the bake.

**serves** 6-8   **prep** 25 min   **cook** 45 min

1 Preheat the oven to 350°F (180°C). Combine the flour, sugar, and cinnamon in a large bowl. Rub in the butter until the mixture resembles coarse breadcrumbs, making sure you leave a few small lumps of butter.

2 For the filling, place the apple pieces in a 9in (23cm) ovenproof dish about 3in (7.5cm) deep. Scatter over the brown sugar, flour, and cinnamon. Toss well to combine. Gently pack the filling into the dish.

3 Dot the filling with butter, then spoon the crumble topping over and spread it out gently. Lightly shake the dish to help settle the topping into an even layer.

4 Bake for 45 minutes, until the top is golden brown and the filling is soft when pierced with a sharp knife. Remove and leave to rest for 5 minutes. Serve warm with cream, if desired. You can store the crumble, covered in the fridge, for up to 3 days.

1¾ cups (250g) all-purpose flour

⅔ cup (150g) superfine sugar

1 tsp ground cinnamon

⅔ cup (150g) unsalted butter, softened and diced

### For the filling

8-10 dessert apples, peeled, cored, and diced into ¾in (2cm) pieces

2 heaping tbsp soft light brown sugar

1 heaping tbsp all-purpose flour

½ tsp ground cinnamon

2 tbsp (25g) butter, softened and diced

heavy cream, to serve (optional)

### Make it vegan

Use an equal amount of vegetable oil spread in place of the unsalted butter.

# Plum and Thyme Galette

Fold over the pastry edges to make this free-form tart—this process helps contain the juices of the sweet, sticky plums. You could also replace the plum with another orchard fruit.

**serves** 6-8   **prep** 20 min, plus chilling and cooling   **cook** 40 min

**1** Sift the flour and sugar into a large bowl and mix well. Rub in the butter until the mixture resembles fine breadcrumbs. Add the salt and water to the bowl.

**2** Use your fingertips to bring the mixture together to form a dough, adding more cold water if needed. Transfer the dough to a lightly floured surface and knead it gently and briefly until smooth. Wrap it in plastic wrap and chill for at least 1 hour.

**3** Preheat the oven to 400°F (200°C). On a lightly floured surface, roll out the pastry to a 12in (30cm) round. Transfer it to a large baking sheet sprinkled with a little water.

**4** For the filling, combine the almonds and 1 tablespoon of the sugar in a bowl. Sprinkle it over the pastry, leaving a 2in (5cm) border.

**5** Arrange the plum slices over the filling in a spiral pattern. Fold the pastry edges over them, pressing down lightly to enclose the filling. Brush the pastry edges with the milk, sprinkle the plums with the remaining sugar, and place the thyme in the center.

**6** Bake in the oven for 35–40 minutes, until the plums are soft and the pastry is golden. Remove from the heat and leave to cool for 10 minutes. Then remove the thyme and serve warm with cream, if using.

1⅓ cups (225g) all-purpose flour, plus extra for dusting

2 tbsp (25g) superfine sugar

½ cup (125g) unsalted butter, chilled and diced

pinch salt

3 tbsp ice water

light cream, to serve (optional)

## For the filling

1 tbsp ground almonds

3 tbsp superfine sugar

1 tbsp milk

3 sprigs thyme

3 large ripe plums, stoned and thinly sliced

### Make it vegan

Replace the unsalted butter with an equal amount of vegetable oil spread, and use soy milk instead of cow's milk.

# Poached Pears in Red Wine

Taking on the rich purple hues of red wine, poached pears are a simple and classic dessert. Here the pears are laced with cinnamon, orange zest, and a little fresh thyme. The flavors deepen the longer the pears are kept in the cooking liquid.

**serves** 4   **prep** 10 min, plus cooling and chilling   **cook** 35–45 min

1   Place the wine, sugar, cinnamon, orange zest, and thyme in a lidded, heavy-bottomed saucepan. Bring to a boil, stirring until the sugar melts. Then reduce the heat to a low simmer.

2   Slice a disk off the base of each pear to allow it to stand upright. Add the pears to the pan, making sure they are submerged in the wine. Cover and cook for 20–30 minutes, until the pears are just soft when pierced with a knife.

3   Remove and cool to room temperature. Transfer the pears and cooking liquid to a large dish and cover with plastic wrap. Chill until needed, or overnight to darken the color. Bring to room temperature before serving. Then discard the cinnamon, orange zest, and thyme.

4   Strain ¾ cup (200ml) of the cooking liquid into a heavy-bottomed saucepan. Bring to a boil, then reduce the heat to a simmer. Cook for 15 minutes, until slightly thickened. Leave to cool until just warm. Place the pears upright on serving plates and pour over a little of the sauce. Serve warm with whipped cream, if using.

2½ cups (750ml) red wine
⅔ cup (150g) superfine sugar
1 cinnamon stick
peeled zest of 1 orange
1 sprig thyme
4 just-ripe pears, peeled
whipped cream, to serve (optional)

# Triple Chocolate Chip Brownies

The best kind of brownie is crisp on the surface and gently yielding on the inside. If you prefer them really soft and gooey, bake them for 5 minutes less than suggested here. If you like them firm, add 5 minutes more to the cooking time.

**makes** 9   **prep** 20 min, plus cooling   **cook** 50 min

1  Preheat the oven to 350°F (180°C). Lightly grease and line an 8in (20cm) square cake pan with parchment paper, leaving some overhang. Melt the butter, dark chocolate, and very dark chocolate in a heatproof bowl over a saucepan of simmering water, making sure it does not touch the water. Stir until smooth, then leave to cool.

2  Gradually add the vanilla extract, superfine sugar, and brown sugar to the mixture and whisk well to combine. Then add the eggs, one at a time, whisking well after each addition until smooth. Place the flour, cocoa powder, salt, and baking powder in a separate bowl and mix well.

3  Use a spatula to fold the dry ingredients into the chocolate mixture and combine until smooth. Then mix in the milk chocolate chips and white chocolate chips until evenly incorporated. Pour the brownie mixture into the prepared pan, and spread it out evenly.

4  Bake for 40–45 minutes, until an inserted toothpick comes out clean. Leave to cool slightly before removing the brownie from the pan. Then cut it into nine equal pieces, cleaning the knife with a damp kitchen towel between cuts. Serve warm with vanilla ice cream, if desired. You can store the brownies in an airtight container for up to 5 days.

½ cup (115g) unsalted butter, plus extra for greasing

6oz (175g) good-quality dark chocolate, finely chopped

2oz (60g) very dark chocolate, at least 85 percent cocoa solids, finely chopped

2 tsp vanilla extract

1 cup (200g) superfine sugar

¼ cup (50g) dark brown sugar, packed

2 large eggs

1 cup (125g) all-purpose flour

3 tbsp natural cocoa powder

¾ tsp salt

¼ tsp baking powder

⅓ cup (60g) good-quality milk chocolate chips

⅓ cup (60g) white chocolate chips

vanilla ice cream, to serve (optional)

### Make it vegan

Replace the unsalted butter with the same amount of vegetable oil spread. Mix 2 tbsp flax seeds with 6 tbsp warm water. Let it sit for 15 minutes and use the mixture in place of the eggs in step 2. For the chocolate and chocolate chips, choose vegan varieties.

# Index

# Acknowledgments

**DK would like to thank**:
DK Australia would like to thank: Lucy Gwendoline Taylor for writing and editing the first chapter of the Australian edition; Sunil Sharma, Pushpak Tyagi, Vikas Sachdeva and Anurag Trivedi from DK India for the internal design; Ella Egidy for the cover design; Niki Foreman for proofreading; and Max McMaster for the index. DK UK would like to thank: Oreolu Grillo and Millie Andrew for editorial assistance.

**Text credits**
Recipe material in this publication was previously published in *Step by Step Desserts* (2015), *Grains as Mains* (2015), *Healthy Gut Cookbook* (2016), *Modern Australian Vegan* (2018), *Pasta Reinvented* (2018), *Plant-Based Cookbook* (2016), *Power Pulses* (2017), *Ramen Noodle Cookbook* (2015), *Sprouted!* (2017), and *The Slow Cook Book* (2018).

**Image credits**
All images © Dorling Kindersley
For further information see: **dkimages.com**

**About the contributor**
Lucy Gwendoline Taylor is a Melbourne-based Accredited Practising Dietitian and Accredited Nutritionist with a special interest in whole food, plant-based diets. Alongside her private practice, Lucy maintains a popular blog (BloomNutritionist. com), which features evidence-based, plant-based nutrition information. She has also written about plant-based diets for online and print media publications, including *The Age* and *The Sydney Morning Herald*. She has been vegan since 2013, and aligns with the vegan philosophy for ethical, environmental, and health reasons.

**Producer** Samantha Cross
**Producer, pre-production** David Almond
**Pre-production manager** Sunil Sharma
**Art editor** Vikas Sachdeva
**Senior DTP designer** Pushpak Tyagi
**DTP designer** Anurag Trivedi
**Jacket designer** Ella Egidy
**Senior editor** Bethany Patch
**Editor** Paige Farrell
**Contributor** Lucy Gwendoline Taylor

**DK UK**
**Editor** Amy Slack
**Senior art editor** Glenda Fisher
**US editor** Megan Douglass
**Jacket designer** Nicola Powling
**Producer, pre-production** David Almond
**Producer** Samantha Cross
**Managing editor** Stephanie Farrow
**Managing art editor** Christine Kielty
**Art director** Maxine Pedliham
**Publisher** Mary-Clare Jerram

First American Edition, 2020
Published in the United States by DK Publishing
1450 Broadway, Suite 801, New York, NY 10018

First Australian edition published in 2019 by DK Australia,
an imprint of Penguin Random House Australia Pty Ltd
707 Collins St, Melbourne, Victoria 3000

A catalog record for this book
is available from the Library of Congress.
ISBN 978-1-4654-9246-3

Printed and bound in China

A WORLD OF IDEAS:
**SEE ALL THERE IS TO KNOW**

**www.dk.com**